Scanning and manipulating images

Olivier Pavie

Prentice
Hall

An imprint of PEARSON EDUCATION

PEARSON EDUCATION LIMITED

Head Office:
Edinburgh Gate
Harlow
Essex CM20 2JE
Tel: +44 (0) 1279 623623
Fax: +44 (0) 1279 431059

London Office:
128 Long Acre
London WC2E 9AN
Tel: +44 (0) 171 447 2000
Fax: +44 (0) 171 240 5771

First published in Great Britain 2000

© Pearson Education Limited 2000

First published in 1999 as
Se Former En Un Jour: Numériser et retoucher ses images
by Simon & Schuster Macmillan (France)
19, rue Michel Le Comte
75003 Paris
France

Library of Congress Cataloging in Publication Data
Available from the publisher.

British Library Cataloguing in Publication Data
A CIP catalogue record for this book can be obtained from the British Library.

ISBN 0-13-025783-4

10 9 8 7 6 5 4 3 2 1

Translated and typeset by Cybertechnics, Sheffield.
Printed and bound in Great Britain by Ashford Colour Press, Gosport, Hampshire.

The publishers' policy is to use paper manufactured from sustainable forests.

Contents

■■

Contents

Introduction

■■■

This book is not intended to turn you into a professional scanner operator: its aim is to guide you when choosing your scanning set up, for home and business use. The book also aims to provide answers to all those questions on how to use the software and get the best from your source material. The main types of problems are covered; allowing you to troubleshoot a substantial number of the problems you may encounter, be they software or source material related.

One final point: this book is divided into twelve chapters, each of which should take no longer than one hour. Don't be put off: it will take you far less than twelve hours to get scanning and retouching!

■ Special icons

On top of text and images, throughout the book you will find icons that indicate a particularly useful byte of information.

 These notes contain definitions, technical detail or other useful information.

 These notes warn you of any problems you might encounter following certain operations. They also tell you what the pitfalls are. Take careful note of these warnings as they will save you a lot of headaches!

 These notes show you shortcuts and help you speed up some tasks.

1 What is scanning?

For many people, a photograph means a camera, transparencies, negatives, prints, enlargements... All of these are more or less involved in scanning; the only difference being that there is an extra ingredient in the mix: the computer, with its endless possibilities for retouching, text insertion, montage, printing... A photograph is turned into an image that a computer can view, copy, print and integrate into any medium: from a printed page to a Web page!

■ Displaying an image on a PC

In order to be displayed on a computer screen, an image must be digitised, in other words turned into digital data that the computer understands. There are many ways to digitise an image. The first is to digitise the image using a scanner, from a reflective (paper), negative or transparent original. There are many types of scanners, each type made for different levels of requirement. Flatbed scanners are mainly used to scan photographs, pre-printed matter, book covers and so on (see Figure 1.1).

A sheet-fed scanner (see Figure 1.2) works somewhat like a fax machine: the photograph or document to be scanned is inserted, and is read and digitised as the original feeds through. This type of scanner has various disadvantages, from the practical (you won't be able to scan anything other than loose sheets) to the technical (risk of paper jams using some types of paper, and distortion of the image).

The other types of scanners are normally for scanning transparencies and negatives, and they are normally much more expensive (see Figure 1.3).

Figure 1.1 A flatbed scanner is used for digitising all sorts of documents, including books and magazines.

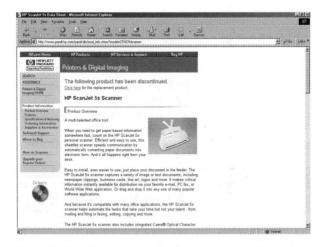

Figure 1.2 Sheet-fed scanners only allow for scanning of loose sheets and photographs.

Figure 1.3 Microtek is one of the market leaders for cost-effective transparency scanners.

■ Digital cameras

Digital cameras, by definition, do not use film: the way that pictures are stored on a digital camera is very similar to how a PC stores data (see Figure 1.4). Images are stored directly as digital data in memory which can take the form of a floppy disk, a hard disk, a flash card or even a chip. The quality of the image is entirely dependent on the quality of the digital camera.

It is worth noting that at the time of writing, digital cameras which can give the same quality as a traditional 35mm camera cost in the region of £10,000! More reasonably-priced digital cameras are aimed at users who just want to cut out the development stage of traditional photography.

In other words, they are aimed at those who love photography without the messy bits. In Appendix A, you will find some useful information to help you chose a digital camera.

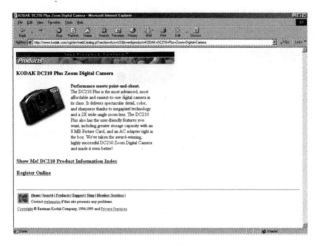

Figure 1.4 A digital camera looks just like a standard camera.

In more detail

The main advantage of digital cameras is: you get instant pictures! You will still need to be able to download the pictures from the camera efficiently. There are two main methods for achieving this. The most used method (and the quickest) is to use a serial cable connected to the serial port on your PC. It's the quickest method because you don't need any special setup to connect the cables, and it is the easiest because all desktop and notebook PCs have a serial port. The second method is to use a digital camera capable of reading a floppy disk. The only problem with this is that it uses an internal reading device that decreases the battery life of the camera. Most other systems, excluding USB (which is very quick and easy to use, but not on all PCs), prove to be unwieldy when downloading data to the PC.

You're going to need these

In order for a camera to compensate for its lack of resolution (as a minimum, go for the camera that can capture at 700×500), it should have a LCD preview screen (mini-screen to be able to preview the image).

The screen will allow you to get the best from your camera. You will be able to see a preview of the picture that you are about to take so you can make all the adjustments necessary. Once you have taken the picture, you will be able to see it instantly, and decide whether to store it or delete it: this lets you delete pictures you are not happy with and helps you save valuable memory. If you can, choose a camera where you can turn the screen off since the preview screen can limit the battery life of the camera.

Integral storage capacity is also a very important feature: try and choose a camera that is able to store about twenty (20) high-resolution pictures (most cameras have high- and low-resolution modes, the exact resolutions vary from one model to another). The lens of the camera is often forgotten on digital cameras, therefore pay particular attention to this item: does it have macro mode so that you can take a good close up, or do you have to be at a certain distance? Macro mode is particularly useful for detail work.

New cameras every day

There are new camera models on the market every day, which makes it difficult to recommend particular models. All you need to be aware of is that the main manufacturers of digital cameras are Kodak, Casio, Konica, Fuji and Agfa.

■ Working with your images

All digital cameras are supplied with software which allows you to download data from the camera to the computer. The actual transfer method varies depending on the camera and the computer, but the end result is the same: display the image on screen and open it with image editing software that has all the various tools necessary for retouching (eraser, paintbrush, spray-can, etc.). These tools give you the ability to change the image at will, until you have either reached the depths of bad taste or produced a masterpiece. All you need is a few clicks of the mouse button and good software!

Some software is task-specific and fairly straightforward whereas the more feature-rich software, which is often more powerful, takes longer to learn to use to best effect.

Figure 1.5 Kai's Power Goo is ideal for caricatures.

■ Having enough colours

In order to be able to work on an image properly, your monitor should be able to display in thousands, or better still in millions of colours. Most PCs made after 1995 (apart from some notebooks) are able to switch to the required colour depth. It is useful for the user to know how to change these settings on their PC. In Windows 95 or 98 you can change the colour depth of the monitor by accessing the Display control panel. Go to the Colors menu and choose the desired colour depth. Don't worry if your choice of colour depth changes the display size, it's just that the memory on the video card (the card inside the PC that controls display functions) is not enough to display both a higher colour depth and maintain the larger display size. See Table 1.1 for a reference guide for resolution and memory. If your display does not fit into any of the parameters listed, it is possible that your display is either poorly set up, or that the video card has incorrect drivers: contact your retailer. If your display only shows 256 colours instead of 65,000 colours or 16.7 million colours, you will be able to tell very easily because your images will not look very good: you will sometimes be able to see bands of colour or tone where the original has shading. Figures 1.6 and 1.7 show exactly this, but colours are replaced by shades of grey.

Table 1.1 Video RAM on video cards and relative display.

Video RAM	Display size	Colour depth
1 MB	640 × 480	16.7 million (65,000 on S3-based video cards)
1 MB	800 × 600	65,000
1 MB	1024 × 768	256
1 MB	1280 × 1024	16
2 MB	640 × 480	16.7 million
2 MB	800 × 600	16.7 million

Video RAM	Display size	Colour depth
2 MB	1024 × 768	65,000
2 MB	1280 × 1024	256
2 MB	1600 × 1200	16
4 MB	640 × 480	16.7 million
4 MB	800 × 600	16.7 million
4 MB	1024 × 768	16.7 million
4 MB	1280 × 1024	65,000
4 MB	1600 × 1200	256

Figure 1.6 An image displayed with 16 levels of grey.

Figure 1.7 The same image displayed with 256 levels of grey.

■ Printing

Having worked on your image, you will want to print it. In order to achieve a high degree of quality you will need to use a photo-quality printer. The paper you use must also be of sufficient quality. There are lots of different types of photo-quality paper available on the market at the moment: prices vary from a few pence per sheet to a few pounds per sheet! Bear in mind that this cost is fairly reasonable when you consider that an A4 enlargement at your local photo-lab will cost you more than a few pounds.... To help you choose your printer, you will find more details in the 'hardware' section of this chapter, pages 34 - 35.

Figure 1.8 The Epson Stylus Photo Ex is a good photo-quality printer.

■ Transmission

Digital technology makes it easy to send your images to the other side of the world. You can use floppy disks or CD-ROMs (if you have a CD writer) to send your pictures or you can attach them to an e-mail if you want to use the Internet. The image must be suited to the transmission method and for its final use. This is achieved by using file conversion methods which allow you to save different formats. For now, it is enough to be aware that an image to be sent via the Internet should be more or less the same quality as an image taken with a digital camera, which is very different to the quality of image that can be achieved by scanning an original photograph. An image meant for the Internet should be between 50KB and 200KB, whereas a full page image in a printed magazine will be somewhere in the region of 60MB, or 300 times the size. It would take approximately 5 hours to transmit an image that size over the Internet with a standard 33.6 connection!

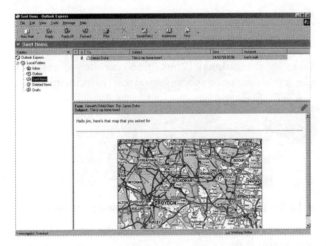

Figure 1.9 Sending a map by e-mail is very useful!

■ Publishing

Images can be published on paper or in the press (if your scanner is of sufficient quality) and on the Internet. In this last case, the publisher of the image must have a website (storage space on a dedicated Web server) or a personal page hosted by the service provider. Most service providers offer free Web space to their subscribers for their own pages. In order to make such a page, you will need an HTML editor and an image editor that can produce Web format images such as JPEG and GIF. Microsoft FrontPage 98 is a good tool for creating Web pages as it combines both intuitive HTML creation as well as Image Composer.

■ In conclusion

Digital photography has many applications, from the more banal to the professional; being able to use the processes will not be a problem once you have grasped the principle.

2 What equipment do you need?

■ ■

Your PC

Monitors

Colour printers

Choosing a scanner

In this chapter you will find information that will help you choose your equipment, if you don't have the necessary tools or want to upgrade your current equipment.

■ Your PC

For digital photography and image manipulation you will need a decent processor, a video card (2D) and RAM: the higher the resolution of the images, the more RAM you will need.

The processor

You will need a fast processor, but that alone will not be enough. Therefore a PC running with an AMD K6-2 at 300 MHz with a 100 MHz motherboard will be quicker than a PC equipped with an AMD K6-2 at 333 MHz and a motherboard running at 83 MHz. The reason why this is so is quite simple: the 333 MHz processor is great for all internal processes, but it doesn't help the peripherals that it drives; these depend on the speed of the motherboard. There may also be other factors to take into account. Therefore, an Intel Celeron processor (first generation) running at 300 MHz on a 100 MHz motherboard will be slower than an AMD K6 running at 233 MHz on the same sort of motherboard, because the Intel Celeron does not have any Level 2 cache.

Figure 2.1 The AMD K6-2 processor is a powerful and cost-effective option.

The AMD K6 processor can have between 256KB and 1MB of Level 2 cache, depending on the amount on the motherboard. On the other hand, it is impossible to install Level 2 cache on a Celeron motherboard. The summary table below will give a you a guide to processor speeds and compatibility.

Table 2.1 Relative performance index on currently available processors

Name	Mfr	Speed	Index
K6	AMD	233 MHz	86
K6	AMD	266 MHz	90
K6	AMD	300 MHz	93
K6-2	AMD	300 MHz	100
K6-2	AMD	333 MHz	110
K6-2	AMD	350 MHz	116
Pentium MMX	Intel	233 MHz	61
Pentium II	Intel	233 MHz	79
Pentium II	Intel	266 MHz	91
Pentium II	Intel	300 MHz	100
Pentium II	Intel	333 MHz	110
Pentium II	Intel	350 MHz	116
Pentium II	Intel	400 MHz	132
Celeron	Intel	266 MHz	64
Celeron	Intel	300 MHz	68
6X86MX	Cyrix	PR233	90
M2	Cyrix	300	99

The indices in Table 1.2 are an indication only and represent the average performance of each processor performing a variety of tasks.

2D video cards

This section deals with 'traditional' graphical applications, as opposed to 3D ones. A video card, or graphics card, must interpret graphical commands sent by the processor to the display. To make even the simplest of boxes in Windows, the processor issues the following instruction to the graphics card: 'draw a white box this size, then draw a grey box and so on.' The delay in the card processor must be very short indeed for the process to appear immediate.

There are three main points that should be considered in 2D graphics: the size of your bus (we have seen the 16-bit bus develop to the 32-bit bus, and then came the 64-bit bus), the clock speed of your bus (the latest PCI/AGP chipsets can work as high as 100 MHz), and, of course, the computing

Figure 2.2 The Matrox Millennium G200 AGP bus. A real treat for image manipulation!

capacity of the graphic processor. A graphics card can be compared with a PC which is dedicated to managing display only; the more powerful the processor, the quicker it processes instructions. Most current graphics processors convert data into 64-bit chunks; some can even go as high as 128 bits. However, the size of the chunks of information that can be processed should not be the only consideration: the internal computing unit in the processor must also be high-performance and optimised, its work frequency high and the graphics card memory effective (graphics cards carry their own RAM which is on average 2 MB in current PCs).

A graphical processor is a chip whose mission it is to interpret graphical information known as polygons. Whilst the central processing unit in a PC (Pentium, Pentium II and so on) is a generic processor which has no real speciality, the graphics processor excels in geometry. Moreover, each graphics processor has its own particular purpose, and is optimised for one or another function. There are, therefore, some differences between graphics processors.

The size of the memory on a graphics card dictates the colour depth and resolution available (see Table 1.1).

Memory (RAM)

RAM is the processor's reserve when under pressure: RAM is where the processor runs the system software, all the programs and all the data which is being processed. The more RAM available to the processor, the faster it will work. RAM doesn't store data once the PC has been switched off, even if the power is cut by a crash. RAM is seated in a specific place on the motherboard (SIMM or ECC seating).

The more RAM there is in the PC, the faster it can process instructions. Access to RAM is instant in comparison with access to the hard drive which is 100 times slower. You could compare this with the Royal Mail not having to deliver mail

Figure 2.3 An ECC SDRAM 168 pin 64-bit memory module.

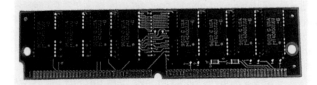

Figure 2.4 A 32-bit 72 pin SIMM.

all over the country but putting all the post in a single letter-box; it would of course mean that the post would be delivered a lot quicker. Speed is also a key factor since RAM is able to process 16 million operations per second. 16 million operations per second doesn't seem a lot when you consider that processors can achieve 400 to 500 million operations per second. This is because RAM, which sits on the motherboard and not on the processor, cannot deal with external operations as quickly as internal ones. DRAM typically has an access time of 60 ns (nanoseconds) and can only operate at a clock speed of 16 MHz (expressed mathematically this would be $1/60^e - 9 = 16.666.666$) when communicating with the processor. The latest generation of RAM, using SDRAM technology has an access time of at least 10 ns and can operate up to a 450 or even 500 MHz clock speed; this, however depends on the motherboard in the PC: the speed of the motherboard dictates the maximum speed of the memory modules.

Hard disks

Memory and disk capacity are often confused with one another. As a rule of thumb, RAM is generally one hundred times less than hard disk storage: RAM is still measured in Megabytes (16, 32, 64, 128MB and so on), whereas hard disks are measured in Gigabytes. A standard medium range PC is normally configured with 32 to 64MB RAM with 4GB of hard disk storage!

How does it work?

The hard drive must be fast enough to work with the processor or else applications will run slowly, especially if there is not a great deal of physical RAM. We have already seen that RAM is the processor's overflow memory; a hard drive completes the picture by being able to provide virtual memory when the processor needs extra memory. This temporary operation is called *disk swapping*. The hard drive is first and foremost a storage medium for non-volatile data: it's on the hard disk of your computer that the system software is installed (DOS, Windows 95, Windows 98 and so on), applications (word processors, scanning software and so on) and all the data that you need every time you use your computer.

Even the best hard drive in the world is still twenty times slower than physical RAM (that's performance for you!); what's more, access speed on a hard disk is measured in milliseconds, whereas memory is measured in nanoseconds (which is 1000 times greater). We haven't yet defined the concepts of access time and output, because they are often not easily understood if taken in isolation. However, we will try and explain the concepts by isolating and discussing them individually.

Access speed is the speed at which the hard drive works when accessing information that the processor needs. A hard disk is a mechanical assembly of a disk (or two or more disks on top of each other) that sits on a spindle. If the required information is at the opposite side of the disk to the reading head (which, incidentally, is made up of several reading heads), the disk has to spin half way round the spindle to present the correct sector containing the information. Access speed therefore depends heavily on spin speed.

Conversely, once the sector is in the correct position, the process of reading the information is very fast. At this stage in the proceedings the speed depends on the number of reading heads and the number of bits a head can read. Other relevant factors are parameters concerning the bus, the processing speed and the cache (cache memory allows you to optimise peripherals).

Figure 2.5 A current 6GB hard drive looks exactly like a 240MB disk did four years ago.

Price range

A good hard drive in the cheaper IDE, EIDE or UDMA ranges can cost between £100 and £200. As far as larger capacity drives go, prices can go up or down from one month to another, depending on the level of manufacture and stocks. SCSI interface disks are a unique case: they can cost up to 30%–200% more than their equivalent IDE capacity. SCSI disks have a higher ROI and they are produced in fewer numbers than other types.

Pointing device (mouse, tablet)

The mouse is not the cursor that you move around on the screen, it is the peripheral that you hold in your hand. Sometimes cursor movements can be somewhat erratic. This can be due to a number of factors: the peripheral you are using is poorly configured or it's of cheap quality, it's old, dirty, not ideal for what you need it for... Mice are not the only pointing devices available: there are also trackballs, tablets and derivatives which are sometimes a mix of the two technologies, as well as touchpads or glidepoints. All these peripherals can be connected to either the serial port or to a PS/2 port on your PC.

Figure 2.6 Microsoft's IntelliMouse.

Suitable peripheral = optimum comfort

Using a suitable peripheral means that you will be using your PC in optimum comfort. If you are not happy with your pointing device, then don't hesitate to change it! The most important thing is to find a pointing device which is best suited to your work on a PC. It should also be ergonomically suited to you: your hand position and finger reach on the buttons must be absolutely comfortable. The peripheral should also be easily accessible and in close proximity to your keyboard in a clutter free area. It should also be properly set up and software-calibrated so that the cursor's screen movements accurately represent your moves with the pointing device, in order to offer the best possible productivity. It should also be a good-quality peripheral.

Quality counts

Many PC resellers supply the cheapest pointing device possible in order to be able to offer competitive pricing. The net result of this is that some users are complaining that they have to change their mouse every three or six months! Even with everyday use for work, play and drawing, two years is the normal life span of a mouse without losing accuracy or having breakdowns. All you need to do is invest wisely (about £40 gets you a good one). Making sure you have a good-quality pointing device (as well as a good monitor, a good keyboard and so on) is making sure that you have optimal comfort whilst working... at least until PCs can be voice controlled (then you will be worried about the quality of your microphone!). How do you know if a peripheral is a good-quality one? Here's a rule of thumb: what is expensive is not necessarily good, but what is good costs more than normal... in computing, price is often indicative of the build quality of the product as well as the quality of the supplied drivers and software. Sometimes the price of high quality materials can reach astronomical heights due to limited production quantities and very high R&D costs.

Pointers

The mouse is most certainly the most widely used pointing device in computing, but it is not necessarily the best: it all depends on how you intend to use the pointer and with which application. The mouse is best used for standard office tasks. There isn't a much better tool for selecting a whole area of text or a print area or even just one word. On the other hand, a mouse is fairly limited when it comes to using drawing software, more limited than a graphics tablet. There are many manufacturers of graphics tablets, amongst which the best are by Wacom and the cheapest by Genius.

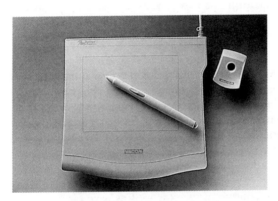

Figure 2.7 A graphics tablet for design and photo-retouching.

Mouse models

The best mice on the market currently, in terms of build and drivers, are those from Microsoft and Logitech. These two manufacturers have worked hard on getting the ergonomics of their products right, in order to make them scroll more smoothly and give you a higher degree of precision. Microsoft offers the IntelliMouse and Microsoft Home models; Logitech's best models are the Mouseman for right-handed people, the Pilot PS/2 for both left- and right-handed people – excellent value for money – and the Mouseman Cordless for those who like to have a wireless workplace (infrared mouse). As far as other manufacturers go, the only real competitor is Mitsumi, who have truly inexpensive peripherals that are of a reasonable quality.

Connectivity

Apart from the standard connectivity offered by your computer through PS/2, serial or parallel ports, it is a distinct advantage if your PC has a USB port.

USB takes the form of a new type of connection on your PC. It has been available for some time on most branded PCs, and it is now supplied on most motherboards, even on entry level PCs.

What is USB? It means *Universal Serial Bus*. In other words the USB is a development of the serial port where you would connect a modem or sometimes a mouse, or, very rarely, another peripheral, (mainly because the serial interface is too slow to support any serious data transfer!). USB has allowed

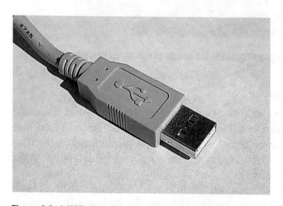

Figure 2.8 A USB plug allows a USB peripheral to connect to the USB port.

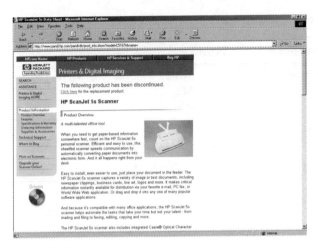

Figure 2.9 The HP ScanJet 5s USB scanner is amongst the first scanners to adopt the USB norm.

the serial port to go from 115 KBits per second to 12 MBits, in other words – in bytes, from 14 KB/s to 1.5 MB/s.

Of course, this is way off the speed of a hard disk, but it's a start! Another advantage of this new standard is that you can daisy chain up to 127 devices on one USB port (obviously connecting 127 devices will have an adverse effect on performance). Other than that, it is a distinctive advantage. Most peripherals no longer need to have a separate power source in order to work: USB supplies the necessary power to most devices. The end of multiple extensions and messy power connectors!

Conclusion

Table 2.2 gives a breakdown of a PC best suited to scanning and retouching.

Table 2.2 Breakdown table for a 'digital workstation'.

Component	Type	Characteristics
Processor	K6-2, 6X86, Cyrix M2, Pentium II	from 333 MHz
Memory (RAM)	32-bit or 72-bit from 64 MB	
Hard disk	E-IDE/U-DMA	from 4 GB
Monitor	SVGA	from 17 inch
Graphics card	AGP	Excellent for 2D, not amazing for 3D, DirectX 5/6 compatible
Ports	USB	Very practical, these ports allow for quick installation of peripherals and hot swapping, without installation problems
Reader	CD-ROM	from 20× or DVD

■ Monitors

The monitor connects directly to the VGA port on the graphics card but it may not be the ideal one both for you or for your graphics card. A quick look at the possible pitfalls will avoid any potential problems and wasting money.

On the one hand there are original equipment manufacturers 'OEMs' (who package a monitor with the PC from manufacture) and on the other hand there are 'after market' ones that are available to add after buying your PC. Monitors which are supplied with the PC are generally not the best ones: they usually fulfil the minimum requirements of the advertised specs of the PC system (in the best scenario). Many users aren't really too concerned with the quality of their display or of other features of their monitor. This is usually because of a lack of understanding.

This lack of understanding normally results in eye strain, poor viewing comfort and a very limited functionality. It's almost as if everyone had portable televisions and ignored all the other sizes available on the market!

Figure 2.10 A 17" monitor has a good viewable size and is ideal for photo-retouching.

What features for which functionality?

Whereas a 36" television will merely enlarge an image in relation to a 14" portable set, larger computer monitors give you not only a larger image but also a much better resolution image and a consistency of image all at the same time. Therefore, a 15" (measured on the diagonal) monitor provides a good picture at a resolution of 800×600 pixels, whereas a 17" monitor gives you a great picture at 1024×768 pixels.

These features allow you to view a picture at a full resolution of 800 × 600 as well as all the palettes and menus in your photo retouching software.

Be aware that if you like the way your 14" monitor keeps the image consistent, you will have to make certain adjustments to keep this consistency when you move up to a higher resolution. You will have to either keep or improve the refresh rate, since the image will be larger, for which you will need a good monitor. If your old 14" monitor displayed 640 × 480 pixels at 75 Hz refresh rate (100 Hz gives excellent image stability), your new 15" monitor should be able to display 800 × 600 pixels at 75 or 80 Hz. The same applies to a 17" monitor displaying at 1024 × 768 pixels. On top of all this, should you want to get the same level of detail on the larger monitor, you should choose a model that has a good dot pitch (the size of the tube footprint) which is the same or less than your original monitor (0.25 mm is better than 0.28 mm), and certainly not more (over 0.3 mm your display will be fairly poor). You will obviously suffer from a high level of discomfort and therefore suffer the financial consequences.

USB monitors

USB monitors have not been around for very long. Even if these monitors let you easily change display characteristics (resolution, refresh rate and so on) since the advent of Microsoft Office, you will find that it is a great advantage to buy a model which has more than one USB port. You will be able to add as many USB peripherals as there are free ports, without the least disadvantage.

Special functions for photo retouching and drawing

Windows 98 (sometimes also Windows 95), provides you with the tools to colour-calibrate your monitor easily. These are called *colour space profiles*. These profiles which come with Windows 98 or even with your monitor, will allow you to match the colours displayed with the printed result. Figure 2.11 shows how to add a colour space profile in the display properties dialog box on your PC.

Figure 2.11 With Windows 98, you can assign a colour profile in the display properties dialog.

Other advantages of a good-quality monitor

Apart from the abovementioned technological advantages offered by these monitors, there are plenty more reasons why you should make sure that you get a good-quality monitor. You can store your settings so that you don't have to modify your settings every time you change resolution; they are automatically recognised by Windows 95 (DDC1 and DDC2) so that they automatically select the best resolution and refresh rate on the basis of the card available; if they are EnergyStar compliant they have energy saving properties and are also low emission (TCO, MPRII compliant).

How much?

Comfort, safety and quality have their price. If a 15" monitor sold with a new PC costs between £100 and £150, branded 15" monitors start at £200 (£250 for better ones). As far as 17" monitors go, some PC vendors market them at £180. Be sceptical about the quality of the monitor: just a good-quality tube can cost as much as £120, and by the time you have added the cost of the electronics, labour, the manufacturer's margin, the distributor's margin and the retailer's margin, £300 should get you a good 17" monitor for general office use, and you will need to pay at least £400 for a graphics or multimedia 17" monitor.

■ Colour printers

In less than two years, advances in colour printing technology have been astounding. Costs have decreased substantially. All of a sudden you can print incredibly good quality colour pictures with a printer costing less than £200!

Less than £200 gets you...

You just wouldn't have imagined it: Hewlett Packard, Canon, Epson and Lexmark have done it, as well as some others; they have managed to make colour printers worthy of the name and able to produce high-quality photo output. Printer manufacturers have managed to get to this level of quality by constantly improving the fineness and quality of the inks, by increasing the number of colours available, striving to improve paper quality, software and so on. Also, given that the basis for print heads is the same as processors (silicon wafers), it makes sense that their evolution followed that of processors. Photos printed on a £200 printer are approximately the same quality as disposable cameras can generate (approximately 800 ASA) – you would only be able to see the grain under a magnifying glass. It would be a fair bet that all photographic prints will be inkjet printed in five years' time!

Printer, paper, cartridges

Good photo-quality printing is a combination of the printer's performance, its print head and the paper used. The printer's performance can be measured in DPI (dots per inch: how many dots there are in an inch). Unfortunately, manufacturer's definitions start becoming a little flexible at this point; users can feel a little lost when they can see that the documentation starts talking about a 300 dpi printer having the same capabilities as a 1200 dpi printer... In actual fact, for various technical reasons (manufacturers don't even talk about the same sort of dots!) the two printers have the same end quality in terms of printing. So that you don't get too confused, ask your vendor to tell you how many nozzles there are on the print head: this will give you a better idea of the quality of the printer... Once you've got all that straight, move on to the cartridges. Some manufacturers only produce some models, whereas others make the whole range: colour cartridges, black only, photo-quality cartridges and so on. The most economical cartridges are the ones that don't have a built-in print head. The most practical are the integrated cartridges: one cartridge does it all. Another headache! There's more... you still need to choose the right paper: coated, ultra-white, matt, glossy... Each make has a different range on offer. You will notice that there are no obvious differences between makes of paper; experiment and try the paper that best meets your needs and that of the printer.

If you still have trouble choosing a printer after all this, then go on the quality of the output samples (just make sure they are from that printer!) and compare them with your original. If you can't compare output, then fall back on the resolution and number of nozzles per print head.

■ Choosing a scanner

Some scanners cost £29.99, others cost more than £200. More professional scanners can cost thousand of pounds! In other words, be careful which you choose, because there's a vast difference in quality!

Basic requirements

There are a couple of things that you should bear in mind with scanners on the general market: connectivity. It is easier to connect a scanner to a printer port than it is to install a special card in your PC. It should be pointed out that the parallel port can sometimes be a little unpredictable, depending on the drivers and the PC type. Having a scanner connected to the printer port will also make it difficult to connect a printer! Moreover, you will not be amazed at the speed of parallel scanners, apart from maybe the HP 5100C which is as quick as the 5P which runs off a dedicated card.

Resolution. Be on your guard if the scanner you are looking to buy offers a high resolution for the money. It may not be the bargain you thought. The higher the resolution, the slower the scanner. Cheap scanners are slow anyway due to the cheaper engines: you can guess what the end result is going to be. A 300 dpi scanner is more than adequate for a wide variety of applications, and is the choice of 99% of non-professional users, the other 1% needing to scan at high enough resolution to find a needle in a haystack... To give you an idea of the quality, a monitor displays at 72 dpi, which is fine for photographs. If a parallel scanner doesn't tempt you and if installing a separate card in your PC seems too much like hard work, why not go for USB? It's a very practical solution but there are two drawbacks. There aren't that many USB scanners out there yet and not all PCs have a USB port to connect to.

Bundled software

The last thing to take into consideration when buying a scanner is to check out the software supplied with it. Buying a scanner is a good way to get hold of some retouching software or OCR (optical character recognition) software for scanning text. Go for scanners that bundle these manufacturers: U-Lead, Adobe, Xerox, Caere, Corel, Micrografx, Microsoft or Live Picture: you will get your money's worth and the software will spur you on to push your boundaries and use your scanner to greater advantage.

It's not unusual for buyers of bargain scanners to complain of poor scan quality: symptoms of which are vertical banding, inconsistent colours and so on. If your bargain scanner isn't from a damaged stock sale or expressly says that it is damaged in some way, ask for a replacement scanner or your money back. If the scanner is an end-of-line model and the vendor no longer sells them, they are nevertheless liable for the period of the warranty.

3 Installing your scanner

■ ■ ■ ■ ■ ■ ■ ■ ■ ■ ■ ■ ■ ■ ■ ■ ■ ■ ■ ■

Check list

Installation and unlocking

Installing a USB scanner

Installing a parallel scanner

Installing a scanner with a proprietary interface

Installing a SCSI scanner

You've just bought your scanner and it is either a parallel, proprietary card, SCSI or USB scanner. In this chapter we will cover all these types of connectivity.

 This chapter in no way replaces the installation guide supplied with your scanner: it should in fact be used in conjunction with the installation guide. In actual fact, manufacturer's manuals often make assumptions and describe some procedures in shorthand, without really taking into account the level of expertise of the user or your particular configuration or the type of problems you might come across. Each type of scanner has its own method of installation, which depends on the type of connection it uses.

■ Check list

Before starting to install your scanner, check that you have all of the following items in the packaging:

- the scanner;
- power cable (except maybe for USB scanners);
- parallel, USB, SCSI or proprietary cable;
- documentation;
- CD-ROM and/or disks with software and drivers;
- interface card (if it is a SCSI scanner or proprietary one);
- a photograph or other means of calibration.

■ Installation and unlocking

This section is relatively short and aims to give you general guidance.

Location

Whatever your scanner type, you will have to place it on a flat, uncluttered surface, close to your computer. You will find that the cables supplied are fairly short anyway and that you will have to find a flat location next to your PC.

Once you have freed up some space, go ahead and locate your scanner. Don't plug anything in just yet.

Unlocking

In most cases your scanner will have a lock-down system which protects the scanning head when moving the scanner around. This system is very easy to unlock once you have found where the mechanism is (normally on the underside of the scanner). Most manufacturers provide a label which gives instructions on how to unlock the scanner, but this isn't always the case. Figures 3.1, 3.2 and 3.3 show the main locking systems in use.

Whatever the type of scanner you have bought, read the instructions carefully before unlocking it. Don't forget that if you need to move your scanner, you will need to lock it down again if you want to avoid damaging the scanning head.

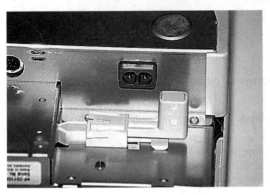

Figure 3.1 The locking system on an HP 5100C doesn't let you plug in the power cable if it isn't unlocked.

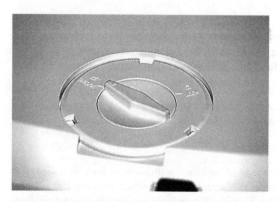

Figure 3.2 Turning the dial locks and unlocks this scanner.

Figure 3.3: This type of scanner is locked with a screw — don't lose it!

■ Installing a USB scanner

The good thing about a USB scanner is that, in theory, you don't need to do much to get it to work. Just plug it in and off you go!

Once you have located and unlocked your scanner, you must connect your scanner to a free USB port on either your computer (see Figure 3.4), a USB hub (see Figure 3.5) or your monitor (if it is a USB monitor and has free ports).

If your scanner has a power cable, then plug this in before plugging in the USB connector.

You can now plug your scanner in on the USB port, even if your computer is switched on: that's what is so great about USB! If everything is OK you will see a dialog box appear (see Figure 3.6).

If Windows cannot auto-detect your scanner, then you will need to insert the driver disk or CD.

Insert the disk or CD and click OK. It may be that Windows can't find the right drivers. In this case, consult the manuals to find out where the drivers are for Windows 95 or Windows 98.

If everything has gone OK, make sure that the scanner is installed correctly. Go to the Start Menu, Control Panels,

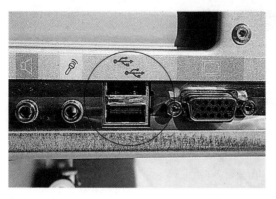

Figure 3.4: Locate a free USB port on your PC, USB hub or monitor.

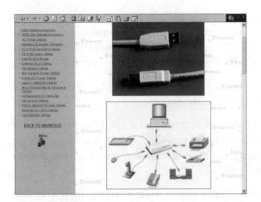

Figure 3.5 A USB hub lets you connect more USB devices.

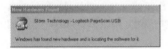

Figure 3.6 The scanner is automatically detected.

Figure 3.7 Your scanner is correctly installed.

System. Look under the Device Manager tab and you should see your scanner appear (see Figure 3.7).

 If your system did not auto-detect your scanner, look in Chapter 6 where you will find a troubleshooting guide.

Once you have finished installing the hardware, move on to installing the software (see Chapter 4).

■ Installing a parallel scanner

Installing a parallel scanner is no more difficult than installing a USB scanner. Problems don't start unless you already have a printer connected to the parallel port and you have to reconfigure your PC to make the scanner work faster or be recognised by Windows.

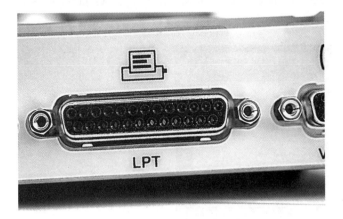

Figure 3.8 Parallel port on the back of the PC.

Windows recognising the scanner or optimisation

This section is optional, unless you can see that the scanner isn't working properly or the manufacturer-supplied driver isn't recognised due to incompatibilities. This section is also for those who want to optimise their PC by speeding up the transfer rates between the scanner and the PC!

In order to fulfil its potential, a parallel scanner needs to have been configured appropriately. ECP handling gives you both performance and compatibility: this standard has been jointly developed by Microsoft (inventor and manufacturer of Windows) and Hewlett-Packard (manufacturer of printers, scanners, PCs and peripherals). With your parallel port set up with ECP handling, you will see transfer rates reach between 1 and 2 MB/s, which is ideal for using a scanner effectively.

To check your parallel port setup, go to My Computer, Control Panels, System. Check in the Device Manager tab, then go down to the header Ports (COM & LPT). Double click on this icon: you will see the box shown in Figure 3.9.

Figure 3.9 The parallel port has ECP handling enabled.

If the dialog doesn't show that the parallel port is in ECP mode, the port isn't properly set up. If this is the case, follow these instructions:

1. Shut down Windows and switch off the computer.

2. Restart the PC and watch for the message 'Press [FX] to Enter Setup' which will appear (the F key mentioned in brackets is the function key that will let you in to your PCs BIOS setup program). Hit the appropriate F key: you will have to get into the PC's setup program. This program holds all the data and hardware setup that controls your PC (see Figure 3.10).

3. Go to the Advanced CMOS Setup menu. Your screen should now be giving you options for 'Parallel Port' or 'LPT Port' followed by 'Normal', 'ECP', 'EPP 1.7' or 'EPP 1.9'. If it isn't already, you need to put the port into 'ECP' mode. Use the keys the program tells you that you can use (normally the cursor keys). If all goes well, then ECP mode is selected and the computer gives it a DMA value. Do not change the value that the computer gives you.

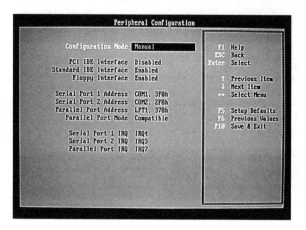

Figure 3.10 The BIOS Setup allows you to program your parallel port (LPT1).

4. Quit this menu (using the Escape key in most cases) and choose Save and Exit Setup in order to save the configuration you have just made.

5. The PC should restart automatically. Windows should then tell you, in the start up screen, that it has found a new ECP port. After having installed the driver, Windows asks you to restart the PC. Click Yes and wait.

6. Then go to Control Panel, System, Hardware and check that Windows has recognised the ECP port.

Straightforward first connection

If you have followed the previous instructions, there is a good chance that your first connection will be problem-free. All you need to do is switch off your PC and connect the parallel cable from the scanner to the PC, making sure that you follow the illustrations on the plugs to see which way round they should be. Once the cable is firmly connected and the power is connected and the scanner is unlocked, switch on the your PC.

Windows should auto-detect the scanner (see Figure 3.11) and ask you for the relevant driver disk or CD-ROM.

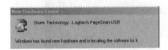

Figure 3.11 Windows has detected a new device, in this case, a Storm Technology scanner.

Connecting your printer at the same time

In order for your scanner and printer to work simultaneously without reconfiguration (that is installing a switch or disconnecting and reconnecting the cables), your scanner should have two parallel ports: one for connecting the scanner and one for connecting the printer (see Figure 3.12).

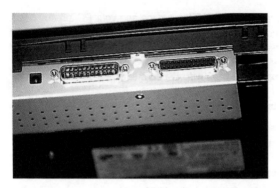

Figure 3.12 A Microtek parallel scanner has two plugs, one for the PC and one for the printer.

So that the printer works perfectly, it MUST be switched on with the scanner before the PC is switched on.

There are some other factors which help the printer to work properly:

- You should use the integral parallel port on your PC and not a secondary one.
- If you are connecting the printer directly to the parallel port, you should install the printer drivers before installing the scanner drivers.

■ Installing a scanner with a proprietary interface

You will have to get into your PC to install the card that comes with proprietary interface scanners: you will have to install it into the slots available on the motherboard. Let's go through the steps necessary to install a card. This operation is quite straightforward and doesn't normally have any associated risks.

If your scanner has a SCSI interface and your PC already has a SCSI card installed, we would recommend you install the card that came with the scanner, keeping the preinstalled one in the computer for the time being. Software bundled with your scanner will normally only work with the card supplied with the scanner.

Getting the PC ready

All new cards and new peripherals that need a controller card installing mean that you will have to get inside your PC.

Your PC and controller cards are 100% Plug and Play compatible

A Plug and Play PC made in 1997 or later (and even some from 1996) makes installing a controller card simplicity itself and doesn't normally involve any problems if the following three conditions prevail:

- The card must be 100% Plug and Play compatible (you can tell from the packaging or from the documentation supplied).

- The PC must not have another card already installed that performs the same function. If the card supplied is a SCSI card, but you already have one installed, you may have some issues: see the section on installing SCSI scanners a little later in this chapter for more details.

- You have Windows 95 or 98 installed.

Your PC and controller card are not 100% Plug and Play

If this is the case, use the following steps:

1. Make sure that you have all the documentation you need and that all the software tools for the new card or peripheral are present.

2. Uninstall all the drivers or software that control the older card which will be replaced, consulting the documentation where appropriate.

3. Follow the installation instructions exactly as they are described in the documentation supplied with the card.

You are now ready to move on to installation.

Installation

Installing a controller card splits into two different steps: hardware and software.

Hardware

You will have to open the PC to install your new card. Make sure you have unplugged the computer from the mains before attempting this. Check your hardware documentation for instructions on how to take the covers off.

Once your PC is open, make sure that there is a free space for your new card. Be careful: if the card is very long you might need to move the cards that are already in the PC. Never install a card where it won't fit properly or straight (the heat sink and fan on a motherboard processor can sometimes cause you to have to move all the cards around).

Make sure that all cards are seated correctly along their whole length (Figure 3.13); it may take a couple of attempts to install correctly, but do not force the card into the slot.

The small piece of metal with the plugs on should fit into a slot at the back of the motherboard. If you can't fit it in there easily make sure that the metal plate is aligned with the slot. If you feel an unusual resistance, check that the metal plate matches the slot perfectly, and that it isn't too big (this can sometimes happen: do not be tempted to file the card to size, it is better to explain the problem to your supplier and try and get a replacement). On some models the expansion slots are on a daughterboard mounted at right angles to the motherboard. If the end piece of the card is disturbed by other cards, then you will have to juggle them about until they fit.

Figure 3.13 The card must be fully seated along all its length.

4. All cards must be secured to the case by means of a screw or whatever the case on your PC lets you use.

5. Sometimes the controller card needs to be connected to another card in your PC by means of a cable. If this is the case, be careful where the cable goes and also how long it is and if it will reach without flexing or pulling the cards it is connecting. If the cable is too short, move the other cards so that the two linked cards sit next to each other.

Software

Once the hardware side of the installation process is resolved, don't close the case up just yet. You might need access to the cards again if the software installation throws up a problem with the physical configuration of the cards. In the meanwhile, reconnect the following:

- power cable;
- monitor power cable;
- monitor cable (which is normally plugged straight into the video card);

- keyboard cable;
- mouse cable;
- scanner cable in to the controller card (don't forget to plug in the power or the transformer for the scanner).

Once all these have been plugged, switch your computer on:

- If your computer doesn't start up, it could be due to many reasons. You may have badly seated the card, or badly reseated a card that you had to move. It may also be that you have an IRQ conflict (interrupt settings). If this is the case you will have to switch the computer off and reset the interrupts manually on the card.

- If your PC starts up correctly first time, then you can proceed to the next stage in the next chapter.

■ Installing a SCSI scanner

If your scanner was delivered with its own SCSI card, and there are no SCSI cards present in your PC, refer back to the previous sections. If you already have a SCSI card installed and you want to add the scanner to the chain of peripherals controlled by the card, read on and find the sections that relate to your situation.

If your scanner came without a SCSI card

This seems to be the norm these days, but the solution isn't as straightforward as all that!

Both your scanner and your controller card must be configured to be able to work together.

Installation and configuration of the scanner

Installing the scanner takes a few steps which you must follow to the letter.

Get a good-quality cable

In order to be able to install a SCSI scanner on a SCSI chain, you will need a cable that will allow you to connect either to the controller card itself or to another peripheral in the chain, such as an external hard drive, external CD-writer and so on. There is more than one type of SCSI standard:

- SCSI-1 (see Figure 3.14);
- SCSI-2 (see Figure 3.15);
- Sub SCSI-2 (see Figure 3.16).

If the items you are trying to connect have different connectors, you can buy cables that have one type of SCSI connector on one end and another type on the other end. Your vendor should be able to help you out with this.

 There are two different formats of Sub SCSI-2. The main one used by brands such as Adaptec or Buslogic is 50-pin Sub SCSI-2. The other format is 60-pin Sub-SCSI-2.

The daisy chaining of SCSI peripherals is illustrated in Figure 3.17.

Figure 3.14 SCSI-1.

Figure 3.15 SCSI-2.

Figure 3.16 50 pin Sub-SCSI-2.

Get the ID right

All SCSI peripherals are identified by their SCSI ID. You can change this number on individual members of the SCSI chain by using the little wheel or push buttons on the back or under the device (see Figure 3.18) including scanners. Numbers go from 0 to 7. Numbers 0 and 1 are normally reserved for the

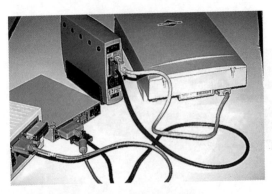

Figure 3.17 Daisy-chaining SCSI peripherals.

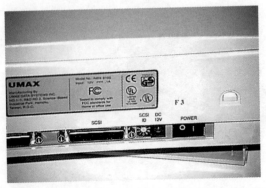

Figure 3.18 A sort of ID wheel which lets you change the SCSI ID of the scanner or of any other SCSI peripheral external to the PC itself.

hard drive and 7 for the SCSI card itself. The other numbers can be assigned to any other peripheral: so long as no two peripherals have the same number.

 Only change the SCSI ID on each peripheral with all power switched off. You should also leave the PC until last after all the peripherals have been switched on.

Don't forget the terminator

For a SCSI chain to work effectively, it must be terminated. Termination is an electrical way of closing the circuit telling the SCSI card that all the peripherals are up and running and ready for use. This is all that is needed to make the SCSI chain active and it can be done in one of two ways: you can install a terminator on the last peripheral in the chain (see Figures 3.19 or 3.20), or you can choose to buy a peripheral which has a terminator built in, normally with a switch called TERM, and moving this to the ON position (see Figure 3.21).

Figure 3.19 Terminator that can be added to the second SCSI port on the peripheral.

Figure 3.20 Terminator that can be used if there are no free ports on the back of the peripheral.

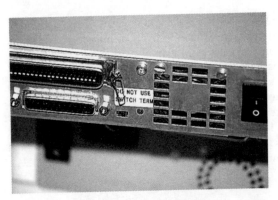

Figure 3.21 Terminator selection in the ON position.

 If the SCSI chain does not include any internal SCSI devices, then termination is not necessary as the card normally takes care of this.

 A problem in the SCSI chain can stop the scanner from working, but at worst can cause data loss on the internal SCSI drive or on a removable SCSI device.

SCSI card configuration

So that a SCSI chain works correctly, you have to set two lots of parameters: on the one hand there is termination (which ensures hardware functionality), and on the other hand parameters which act on communication between devices.

Card termination

A SCSI card which is meant to handle more than one type of SCSI device (in contrast to proprietary ones which come bundled with some scanners) can be set up to auto-terminate in order to ensure that the chain is functional.

Termination on the card must be active if devices in the SCSI chain are:

- exclusively internal devices;
- exclusively external devices.

Termination on the card must not be active if there is a mixture of the above in the SCSI chain.

If you have an Adaptec SCSI card, you can access the setup menus by hitting Ctrl+Q or Ctrl+A on startup, just after the SCSI card is detected (a message to this effect is displayed). You should get the screen displayed as shown in Figure 3.22.

By choosing the card configuration option, you will get to the screen in Figure 3.23.

In the main menu change the termination mode to ON (activate) or OFF (inactive), according to your needs.

If your SCSI card is not an Adaptec branded card, then consult the documentation supplied with the card to determine how to alter the termination parameters.

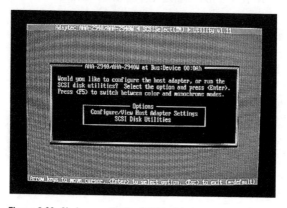

Figure 3.22 Choices available with the Adaptec setup software.

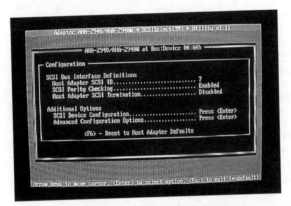

Figure 3.23 Configuration screen of an Adaptec SCSI card.

Other necessary configurations

Some scanners work straight away in a SCSI chain without having to make any further changes to the settings that we have already discussed. On the other hand, some SCSI scanners can throw up problems which appear to be impossible to resolve. If you don't want to run that risk, follow the instructions laid out here and you will only have to change the configuration of the card once, whatever the scanner.

We must change the configuration of the SCSI card. Let's assume that we have an Adaptec card: use the instructions given earlier to get to the configuration screen. Select SCSI Device Configuration: you should see the screen as in Figure 3.24.

Remember that you have changed the ID of your scanner with the ID selector wheel? You will have to enter that same number into the configuration manually:

- Initiate Sync Negotiation: No.
- Maximum Sync Transfer Rate: 5 MB/s.
- Enable Sync Disconnection: Yes.

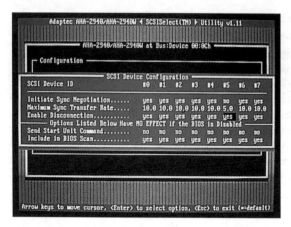

Figure 3.24 SCSI Device Configuration screen of an Adaptec card.

Quit the configuration program after you have saved the settings and your PC will reboot.

If the card you are using is not an Adaptec card, then consult the documentation supplied with the card for the values to input.

Installing SCSI card and scanner drivers

If your SCSI card was correctly installed and all the steps you have taken have been successful, Windows will auto-detect your scanner and prompt you to insert a disk or CD-ROM with manufacturer supplied drivers. Refer to your documentation for installing scanner driver. If Windows has recognised the card but not the scanner, you need to reinstall the card, referring to the section called 'Installing a scanner with a proprietary interface'.

If Windows has detected the scanner, move on to software installation for your scanner, as explained in Chapter 4.

The card bundled with the scanner is different to the one you are already using

This is generally the most problematic case, mainly because the software and drivers supplied with the scanner are specifically tailored for the card bundled with it. As a consequence, the user acquiesces and installs the supplied card and its relevant drivers. This may not have any consequences as far as hardware goes, but from a software standpoint it can conflict with all sorts of devices, from internal hard drives to external peripherals. Conflicts of this nature can prevent the PC from actually starting up.

The best solution is to retrace your steps, remove the bundled card and purchase a cable that will allow you to connect the scanner to the SCSI chain. Have a look at the section called 'If your scanner came without a SCSI card'.

4 Installing the software

In Chapter 3, you installed your scanner and installed the software drivers for it. All you need to do now is install the software that will allow you to use the scanner.

■ Step by step

Make sure you follow the instructions in the manufacturer's *Installation Guide* when installing bundled software. Software installation shouldn't be a problem, if the hardware has been successfully installed. Sometimes, however, Windows does detect the scanner on startup, but fails to find the manufacturer's driver on the disk or CD-ROM on insertion when prompted to do so by Windows.

This can be due to a couple of reasons; the bundled drivers can be either Windows compatible and therefore easily recognised by Windows, or as a program to be run under Windows. In the first case the scanner is auto-detected and Windows displays the message 'scanner XXX on port YYY'. In the second instance, Windows tells you it has found an unknown device.

Don't worry if you get a message auto-detecting the scanner or recognising an unknown device, this is a good sign and you will be able to finish setting up your scanner and use it in minutes. On the other hand, if you get no message whatsoever, then it is time to start asking yourself why. If this is the case go back to the previous chapter and make sure that the hardware is correctly installed.

■ Installing the Twain driver

Correctly installing the hardware driver and getting it recognised doesn't necessarily mean that the scanner will work straight away. You will need a further driver to proceed: the

Twain driver. This is the connection between your software (retouching software, OCR software and so on) and the scanner. This program holds all the information pertinent to the scanner, including all the available options (size, resolution, colour depth, transparency mode and so on). Note that the Twain driver needs the hardware driver in order to make the scanner work.

Refer to Figure 4.1 to gain a better understanding of what Twain drivers can do.

 All Twain compatible software available on the market will allow you to get the best from your scanner: if the software you have is not Twain compatible, it's probably three or four years old and you should get hold of some later versions of the software.

Figure 4.1 The Twain driver on an HP 5100 C scanner.

Not all drivers look the same. They do, however, have the same functionality and use. A Twain driver is a program in its own right and has its own interface. It's almost impossible to use a Twain driver on its own, without going through another piece of software, such as retouching software, or OCR software.

Use the disk or CD-ROM supplied by the manufacturer to install the Twain driver. Table 4.1 shows the name each manufacturer gives to their drivers.

Table 4.1 Manufacturers and their respective Twain drivers

Manufacturer	Name of Twain driver
Agfa	FotoSnap (basic version), FotoLook (professional version)
Hewlett-Packard	PrecisionScan
Microtek	ScanWizard
Mustek	Scanning Desktop

Installing a scanner from 3.5" disks

Even though scanners supplied with 3.5" disks are becoming rarer, you should know how to install from these.

More often than not, the manufacturer labels the first disk 'Run (or launch) Setup.exe (or Install.exe)'. At this point you can do one of two things:

- The first is to double click on My Computer, then on the floppy disk icon. In the next window, double click on Setup.exe (see Figure 4.2): this will start the installation.

- The second option is to go the Start menu, Run and enter a:\setup.exe (see Figure 4.3) in the empty field.

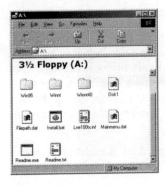

Figure 4.2: Launching the program from the My Computer window.

Figure 4.3: Do it another way: the Run command.

In either case, after you have started the installation process, just follow the on-screen instructions and insert disks as and when prompted to do so.

Installation from CD-ROM

Installation from CD-ROM is very straightforward: simply insert the CD-ROM and an installation menu will display (it is possible that the menu displayed gives multilingual choices).

If the program does not autorun, you can always launch it manually. Just like the floppy disks, the CD holds a program called either Setup.exe, Install.exe or Cdsetup.exe which starts the installation. Here are two methods to find the program:

Figure 4.4: Example of autoplay on an installation CD-ROM.

- Go to the Start menu, Programs, Windows Explorer, then find the CD-ROM (see Figure 4.5) and then search the contents to find the installer program.
- Double click the CD icon under My Computer (this will normally launch the CD installation program), and if a window displays, search through for the installer program.

Whatever method you use, consult the documentation supplied with the scanner to establish the name of the software you need.

By pressing CAPS LOCK or SHIFT when inserting the CD, you will temporarily disable autostart functions.

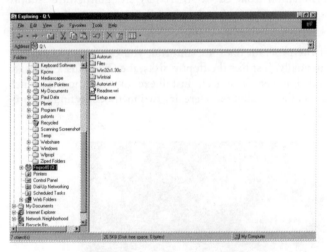

Figure 4.5: Search through the CD-ROM from Windows Explorer.

Installation options

The installation program gives you several options, the first of which asks for the model of the scanner you wish to install.

Manufacturers often put all drivers and software for their range of scanners onto one CD. Make sure you have the scanner model to hand so you can select it from the list available.

The installation program will then ask you what sort of interface you are using. There are multiple versions of some scanners: parallel, SCSI, or USB. It is on installation that you have to define the type of scanner that you have (see Figure 4.6).

Finally, the installation program asks for a directory path for installation (directory, sub directory and so on). You may

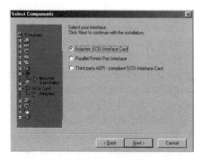

Figure 4.6: Make sure you choose the connection method that corresponds to your scanner.

Figure 4.7: Choose the default path that the installation program gives you.

choose to select your own path or stick with the default path selected by the program, but in any case, make sure you make a note of it, in case you need to find it in order to make sure everything has installed correctly.

■ Installing all the different software

We have already covered all the different types of software you can get with your scanner including retouching and OCR software.

The next section includes the main functions of scanning software to help you find your way around all these different types of software bundled with your scanner. If you want a more in-depth look at the various functions full versions of the software have (as opposed to the bundled versions which are often light versions), skip to Chapter 12 which looks at the main ones on the market. Table 4.2 also shows which software category different bundled scanner software falls into. This information will allow you to install the programs that you need and if you haven't already bought your scanner, be able to make an informed choice on the basis of the bundled software.

Table 4.2 Product name, publisher and main purpose

Name	Publisher	Type
iPhoto Express	Ulead	Retouching
Omnipage LE	Caere	Character recognition (OCR)
PhotoDeluxe	Adobe	Retouching
Photoshop	Adobe	Retouching
Picture-It	Microsoft	Retouching

Name	Publisher	Type
PhotoPaint	Corel	Retouching
TextBridge	Xerox	Character recognition (OCR)
Paint Shop Pro	JASC	Retouching
Photo Impact	Ulead	Retouching
Graphics Suite 2	Micrografx	Retouching
EasyReader	Mimetics	Character recognition (OCR)

Retouching or image manipulation software

We will take an in-depth look into retouching software later in the book. For now all we need to know is that the software lets us draw, scan (with the Twain driver), manipulate the

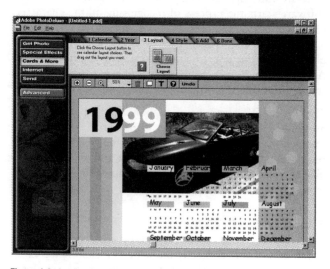

Figure 4.8 A calendar created with Adobe's PhotoDeluxe.

images, rotate them, apply filters to them, clone areas to other scanned images and so on. The differences in the software can be seen by the number of filters available, the number of automated tasks which let you work quicker and more efficiently, colour matching between the screen and the printer. Some software goes much further than simply letting you manipulate images. They have templated greeting cards, calendars, and all sorts of other documents which you can edit and customise using your own images; you can change the colours and the text, and preview the results all in the matter of a few clicks of the mouse.

Optical Character Recognition (OCR) software

The name of the software says it all, this is software which will scan text and recognise it as text, not just an image. You might, for example, want to include an article from a magazine in your archives: all you need to do is open the OCR software and start scanning. Once the image is on screen, the software starts the process of recognising all the characters. Once recognition has been achieved, the text can be edited in a word processing package such as Word. You would then be able to paste this directly into a document you have created. All this will have taken minutes to achieve, whereas a person typing this same text would have taken much longer.

The main differences between bundled and commercially available software – often at a higher price – are that the cheaper ones will not be able to handle multiple column text, recognise as many fonts or be as quick and will also not be able to build profiles and dictionaries according to the parameters you have set.

Installing different programs

Whatever the medium used, floppy disk or CD-ROM, installing software is exactly the same as installing the Twain driver as described earlier in the chapter. If it's on floppy disks, the installation will take place in a certain order, often numbered on the disks. On CD-ROM, installation is carried out via a menu. Using the on-screen menu you can either choose whatever options you need to install the software for each program you want, one after the other, or select everything you need in one go (see Figure 4.9).

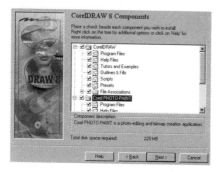

Figure 4.9 Here you can select and install everything you need at the same time.

5 First scan: knowing what to do

■ ■

Starting the retouching software and
configuring the Twain driver

The first scan

The software is installed, the scanner seems to be connected: now is the time to look at what the scanner can do for you.

■ Starting the retouching software and configuring the Twain driver

Before you continue, and so you can make better use of the software, you should configure the OCR or retouching software by telling it which Twain device it will be using.

We will show you how to approach configuration for some of the most popular software.

 *Twain 32 or **Twain 32-bit** drivers are for use under Windows 95 or Windows 98. **Twain 16** or **Twain 16-bit** are the only Twain drivers you can use with Windows 3.1.*

Configuring Adobe PhotoDeluxe

Launch Adobe PhotoDeluxe, then go to the File menu, Open special, Scanner (see Figure 5.1).

The menu that appears will give you the choice of Twain that corresponds to the scanner you are using (see Figure 5.2). In the example shown in Figure 5.2, we have selected the ScanWizard (32-bit) driver for a Microtek scanner and we have clicked OK.

The Twain driver will then launch and give you all the options you need to operate the scanner.

Configuring iPhoto Express

Launch iPhoto Express, then go to the File menu, Acquire, Choose source.

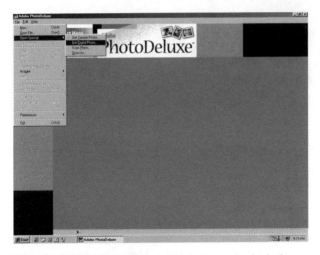

Figure 5.1 In Adobe PhotoDeluxe, access to the scanner is via the
File menu, Open Special, Get Digital Photo.

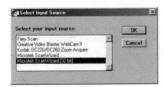

Figure 5.2 Choice of Twain with Adobe PhotoDeluxe.

Figure 5.3: Choice of Twain in iPhoto Express.

The menu that appears will give you the choice of Twain that corresponds to the scanner you are using (see Figure 5.3). In the example shown in Figure 5.3, we have selected the ScanWizard (32-bit) driver for a Microtek scanner and we have clicked Select.

The Twain driver will then launch and give you all the options you need to operate the scanner.

Configuring Corel PhotoPaint

Launch Corel PhotoPaint, then go to the File menu, Acquire, Choose source (see Figure 5.4).

The menu that appears will give you the choice of Twain that corresponds to the scanner you are using (see Figure 5.5). In the example shown in Figure 5.5, we have selected the ScanWizard (32-bit) driver for a Microtek scanner and we have clicked Select.

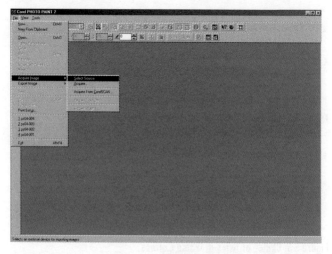

Figure 5.4 In Corel PhotoPaint, access to the scanner is via File menu, Acquire, Select Source.

Figure 5.5 Choice of Twain with Corel PhotoPaint

The Twain driver will then launch and give you all the options you need to operate the scanner.

Configuring Paint Shop Pro 5

Launch Paint Shop Pro, go to the File menu, Import, TWAIN, Acquire (see Figure 5.6).

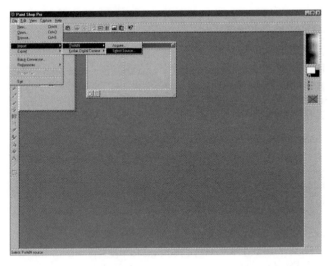

Figure 5.6 In Paint Shop Pro, access to the scanner is by selecting the File menu, Import, TWAIN then Acquire.

Figure 5.7: Choice of Twain with Paint Shop Pro.

The menu that appears will give you the choice of Twain that corresponds to the scanner you are using (see Figure 5.7). In the example shown in Figure 5.7, we have selected the ScanWizard (32-bit) driver for a Microtek scanner and we have clicked OK.

The Twain driver will then launch and give you all the options you need to operate the scanner.

Configuring Picture-It

Launch Picture-It, then go to the File menu, Scan image.

The menu that appears will give you the choice of Twain that corresponds to the scanner you are using. All you have to do to start scanning is to click on the scan button at the bottom of the dialog.

Picture-It is different to the other scanning packages in that it gives you two choices: 'auto-scanning' where the software makes all the decisions for you simply by clicking scan, and a custom scanning mode, which lets you make all the settings and selections you want for scanning.

Configuring Adobe Photoshop

Launch Adobe Photoshop, then go to the File menu, Import, TWAIN_32.

The menu that appears will give you the choice of Twain that corresponds to the scanner you are using (see Figure 5.9). In

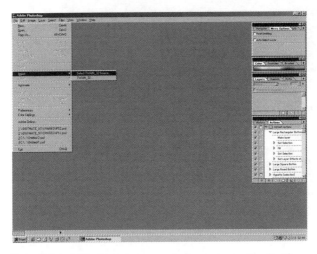

Figure 5.8: In Adobe Photoshop, you select your scanner by choosing File menu, Import, Select TWAIN_32 Source.

Figure 5.9: Choosing a Twain driver in Adobe Photoshop.

the example shown in Figure 5.9, we have selected the ScanWizard (32-bit) driver for a Microtek scanner; all you have to do to start scanning is to click on the scan button at the bottom of the dialog.

The Twain driver will then launch and give you all the options you need to operate the scanner.

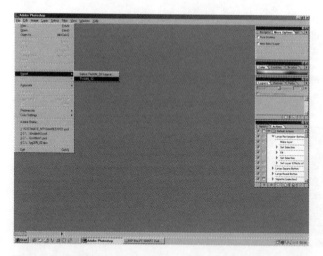

Figure 5.10: In Adobe Photoshop, access to the scanner is by choosing File menu, Import, TWAIN_32.

Rule of thumb

As a rough guide, in current software the Twain driver can generally be found by referencing the File menu, and then a submenu that is linked to scanning, acquiring, source selection and so on.

When you Quit the software, it should remember the last parameters which were set, so you shouldn't have to reset them next time you use the scanner.

■ The first scan

Whatever the software you are using, the Twain driver will automatically execute on the settings you made the second you click on Scan. The user interface is therefore dependent on the make of the scanner, not the software. In order to help you with your first scan, we have chosen an interface that includes all the available options that you are likely to come across with scanners that are currently on the market.

Step one: the document and the scanner

Where you put the document you are about to scan depends on the make of the scanner. We will describe all the relevant procedures for loading an original in the following sections.

Flatbed scanners

If you have a flatbed scanner you will have to lift the lid and place the document scan side face down on the glass, just like a photocopier (see Figure 5.11).

Figure 5.11: Place the scan side face down on the glass.

The top left corner of the document should be placed at the origin 0,0 (see Figure 5.12); this position will vary from scanner to scanner.

Once the document is firmly in place, close the lid gently so that the original is not disturbed.

Figure 5.12: The top left-hand corner of your original must always be at 0,0.

Sheet-fed scanners

If you have one of these, then you will insert the document the same way as you do in a fax. The document should be scan side down and the leading edge is placed into the document feed (see Figure 5.13).

 Documents you feed into a sheet fed scanner should be in good condition – they shouldn't be torn or cut in a hurry. They should also be a minimum of 10 × 5 cm.

Figure 5.13: In a sheet fed scanner, the document is fed in gradually.

35mm transparency scanners

As with a 35mm projector, a 35mm transparency scanner needs to have the slides inserted in the appropriate slot. They should also be pushed home in the scanning module. If you wish to scan negatives, or film strip positives, you should use the holder supplied, without which you will damage the scan head on the scanner.

Step two: prescanning

Now that the original you want to scan is in place, you should perform a prescan. To achieve this, click on scan, this will launch the Twain driver scanning module. Table 5.1 shows where the scan function is located in the main retouching packages.

Table 5.1 Where to find the scanning function in popular software

Software	Access to scan function
Adobe PhotoDeluxe	File, Open Special, Scan a picture (then choose scanner)
Adobe Photoshop	File, Import, TWAIN 32
Corel PhotoPaint	File
Jasc Paint Shop Pro	File, Import, Twain, Acquire
Microsoft Picture-It	File, Scan image (mode 'custom scanning mode'), Scan button
Ulead iPhotoExpress	File, Acquire, Image

A prescan gives an overview of the document you wish to scan which allows you to select the specific area you need to scan. This step is done by selecting Prev in our example (see Figure 5.14).

Figure 5.14 The Prev or Preview button gives you an overview of the document.

 Microsoft's Picture-It has a function which cuts out the configuration stage of the Twain driver. If this is happening, then check in 'scan picture' that you have custom settings selected and not autoscan.

Step three: select the scan area

Once the image is displayed on the screen, you can select exactly which area to scan, by dragging a marquee around it. The procedure to achieve this is nearly always the same:

1. Click into the prescan area and a selection box will appear.
2. With the mouse, click and drag diagonally to enlarge the selection until you have all that you need inside it.
3. Move the marquee selection into the required position. Figure 5.17 shows a defined area in the prescan window.

Step four: start scanning

The selection you have made tells the scanner exactly which area to process. Click on the scan button to start scanning.

You will normally get a progress bar to show that the scanner is working.

Figure 5.15 The selection has been adjusted from the selection in Figure 5.14.

When the defined area has finished being scanned, the resultant image is displayed in the normal retouching software (see Figure 5.16).

Figure 5.16 Only the selected area has been scanned.

Step five: saving the scan

The scanned document is displayed on screen but it is only in the computer's RAM, and therefore not permanent. In order to save it to the hard drive you must go to the File menu and choose Save As. In the dialog box that you get (see Figure 5.17), give the file a name by typing it into the blank area and then click Save.

Figure 5.17 Give your file a name.

Note that in the example in Figure 5.17, the dialog box states 'Photoshop (*.PSD, *.PDD)' next to the save as option. This is the file type that we want to select: for this purpose we have saved it as a native Photoshop format. Most software defaults to its native format when saving. This isn't to say that this format is the one you want or indeed is compatible with the rest of the applications you want to use the image with: in fact you will only be able to use the image with the software that created it if you save it in native format. Happily, as you will see later, each package actually has multiple format options for you to choose from, so that you can save them for use on the Web or in a document or whatever you need it for.

6Troubleshooting

My scanner doesn't work

My scanner works under Windows 3.1, but not under Windows 95 or 98

My PC hangs when I use the scanner

The scanner prevents the printer from working

■ ■

Is your scanner not responding? Does your software not recognise the scanner? This chapter will help you resolve the most common problems.

■ My scanner doesn't work

Possible reasons:

- The scanner is incorrectly plugged in.
- The interface card is not properly configured.
- The scanning software is not properly configured.

The scanner is incorrectly plugged in
Hand scanners

Many hand scanners rely on their connection to the interface in the PC for their power. It is very straightforward to diagnose this problem: either the scanner is plugged in or it's not. If you haven't changed the setup, it is possible that the interface card has become unseated if you moved the PC.

Hand scanners which are connected to the serial or parallel port rely on a separate power supply from a small transformer. Make sure the transformer is connected and that the scanner is switched on.

Flatbed, sheet-fed or transparency scanners

These scanners can be connected to either parallel or serial ports, specific interface cards, or a SCSI card. In all these cases, they are powered either by a transformer or directly from mains power (220V). Make sure the scanner is connected to the PC correctly and that the scanner is switched on.

All scanners that draw their power from outside the PC via a transformer or directly from the mains, need to be switched on before the PC. Moreover, if it is part of a SCSI chain, you should power on all the external devices (hard drive, scanner, SyQuest or other backup) before the PC.

The interface card is not properly configured

It may well be that the problems you are experiencing relate to the interface card being badly setup in terms of either software or hardware.

An interface card relies on IRQs or interrupts. These must be unique and not have the same address as any other card or ports on the PC, or the result will be conflicts and the item will not work. Consult your documentation to understand how to change IRQs and set the card up.

If the scanner is connected to a SCSI card, you will have to make sure the address and interrupts are resolved, but also make sure that you have configured the software appropriately to the card you have. Arm yourself with the card documentation and keep the following in mind when changing the parameters and ID on the scanner (0 to 7):

- Never exceed a throughput of 5 MB/s (5 megabytes/second);
- Use asynchronous transfer.

Your scanner should now work, unless the problem is related to the driver.

For parallel port scanners, the problem is often that the port has not been configured either as bi-directional or as ECP (ECP is the preferred configuration). You will have to get into the BIOS setup to sort this out (see Chapter 3). For USB scanners, make sure that the version of Windows you are using recognises USB (see the section on Installing a USB scanner, page 42).

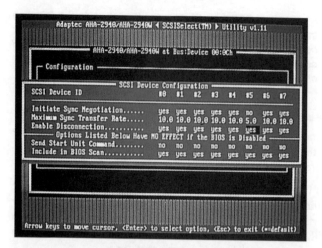

Figure 6.1 This figure shows how to change the parameters to set the SCSI ID to 5 on an Adaptec card.

The scanning software is not properly configured

Most scanners are bundled with a Twain driver that handles the scanner directly and works with drawing software, scanning software and OCR software (iPhoto Express, Corel PhotoPaint, Easy Reader, OmniPage and so on). When launching the software you need, there must a be a way to launch the Twain driver. The first time you do this, the software will ask you to tell it which scanner it should be working with: don't get this wrong because your system will most likely hang otherwise. If you really get it wrong, then you should reinstall the driver and/or the software.

Some Twain drivers actually ask you to define the address and IRQs for the scanner. Be careful when inputting these, as they must be exactly as they are set on the interface card. Some cards are configurable by software, but most require a certain amount of manual intervention on the hardware, to change the position of the jumpers. Always consult your documentation thoroughly before making any changes at all.

■ My scanner works under Windows 3.1, but not under Windows 95 or 98

Possible reason:

- Check the connection.
- The scanner is conflicting with another device.
- Your Windows 95/98 driver is not up to date.
- SCSI scanner: a driver that was necessary for Windows 3.1 is no longer necessary under Windows 95/98.
- The SCSI card needs to be reconfigured.
- Your SCSI card doesn't work with Windows 95/98.

Check the connection
Before doing anything else, always check your connections to make sure all cables are properly seated.

The scanner is conflicting with another device
Everything was fine under Windows 3.1, but all of a sudden you find that Windows 95 or 98 handle conflicts a little differently. In actual fact, when Windows finds that a device conflicts, it chooses stability over anything else and will only handle the devices that were installed at the start. In order to sort this out you will have to go to My Computer, Control Panels, then System.

As a rule, Windows 95 doesn't see scanners as standard devices, but as unknown devices (apart from in some instances, especially in the case of Hewlett Packard scanners; HP supplies a configuration software that is accessible directly from the control panels). Select unknown devices: your scanner should be somewhere in the list. If there is a conflict, the scanner will have a red cross next to it, and you can click on the properties button to see exactly what the origin of the conflict is. Ask yourself if it is simpler to change the setup of the interface card or the other device it is conflicting with (always choose the simpler option).

If your scanner is not seen as an unknown device, it is because it is connected to a SCSI card. Find the list that holds SCSI devices and make sure there is no conflict. If there is a conflict, proceed as previously discussed

Your Windows 95/98 driver is not up to date

It may well be that the Twain driver that worked perfectly under Windows 3.1, no longer functions correctly under Windows 95/98. If this is the case, ask your retailer or the manufacturer for the latest version of the driver (if you are in a hurry, it may be quicker to download it from the Internet).

SCSI scanner: a driver that was necessary for Windows 3.1 is no longer necessary under Windows 95/98

We have come across many cases where a driver that was previously necessary under Windows 3.1 is no longer needed under Windows 95/98, and even stopped the scanner from working correctly or being detected (Agfa, Hewlett Packard and so on). If this is the case, you will have to edit the CONFIG.SYS file.

In Windows 95/98, you should go to the Start menu, select Run and then type SYSEDIT and click OK. All the configuration files the PC uses will appear. Select the CONFIG.SYS window and look for a command line that starts with DEVICE= or DEVICEHIGH= and contains a reference to HPSCAN; SCSISCAN should already be present (check the exact designation in your scanner documentation). If this line is present, make it into a remark by typing REM followed by a space at the beginning of the line, save the changes and reboot the PC. If the line is not there, then the problem lies elsewhere.

We have also come across a case with an Agfa scanner, where the driver was not loaded on startup, but when the Windows launched. The answer here is to delete the driver from the directory it is in (just do a search under Windows to see where the file is), even if the result is that an error message is posted when Windows starts saying something like 'Cannot find XXXX program'.

The SCSI card needs to be reconfigured

Just as in the 'My scanner doesn't work' section, you will have to reconfigure the card until it works with Windows.

Your SCSI card doesn't work with Windows 95/98

Either the card is not Windows 95/98 compatible, in which case it would be better to buy another one (SCSI cards that are bundled with scanners sometimes are highly incompatible with Windows 95/98, or the DOS drivers which are loaded outside of Windows 95/98 to make the SCSI card work are

Figure 6.2 The SCSI driver doesn't seem to work.

out of date). If this is the case, make sure you know what type
of card it is and ask the retailer for the latest DOS drivers.

■ My PC hangs when I use the scanner

Possible reason:

■ The interface card is badly configured.
■ The driver is the wrong type.

The interface card is badly configured

This problem is often due to an IRQ or address conflict
between the card and another card or device in your PC.
Check which device or card it is that is conflicting and
change the address or IRQ appropriately. This sort of problem can show itself in several ways, amongst which: the PC
may display a message such as 'Error in module VxD XX', or
Windows might bomb out and be replaced by a DOS screen,
or might just reboot automatically.

The driver is the wrong type

Either the driver is not the right type for the scanner, or it
isn't compatible with the system, or it's badly set up. Refer to
the section entitled 'My scanner doesn't work' for help in
resolving the problem.

■ The scanner prevents the printer from working

If you have a parallel scanner and the printer hangs directly
off it, this may well be the cause of the problem. Check that
you have the connections the right way round. Also, don't
forget that the scanner needs to be switched on for the print-

Figure 6.3 A parallel scanner may have an extra port to attach a printer.

er to be able to work: to try and isolate the problem, switch everything off, shut down the computer, then switch on the scanner and the printer and finally switch on the PC.

 Always use the original parallel port on the PC and not another port you have added.

7
Changing the scanner, monitor and graphics card settings

■ ■

Image resolution
Colour depth
Pixel per inch

As you have already noticed, the Twain driver you have just used to achieve your first scan, calls for adjustments in *resolution*, *colour depth* and so on. It isn't always easy to get the hang of all the ins and outs of these adjustments. And that is why we will be dedicating this entire chapter to precisely this subject.

■ Image resolution

Image resolution corresponds to the number of horizontal and vertical points (pixels) that make it up. An image which is 800 × 600 pixels is 800 points horizontally and 600 points vertically; the same can be said of a screen which has been configured to 800 × 600 (see Figure 7.1).

If you want to view an image at 800 × 600 when your screen is set to 640 × 480, the image will be cropped top and bottom. Conversely, if the image resolution is 640 × 480 and you display it on an 800 × 600 screen, not all the screen is taken up.

Figure 7.1 The control panel lets you make changes to the screen configuration.

■ Colour depth

There is a difference between the number of colours that your screen can display and the number of colours that makes up the displayed image.

How many colours?

A scanned image in true life colour is made up of 16.7 million colours. For this type of image to be displayed accurately, the screen must be configured to display 16.7 million colours. If the monitor is set to 256 colours, you will see one of two things: either the image will be of such poor quality that tints will be banded and the colour will not correspond to the original (see Figure 7.4), or the image will be pixelated and will be very low resolution (see Figure 7.5). If you only work in 256 colours, then you should save your images in 256 colours. Figure 7.6 shows an image with 16.7 million

Figure 7.2 An 800 × 600 image displayed on a screen set at 800 × 600.

colours which has been optimised to 256 colours and displayed on a 256 colour display. Even though it is far from perfect, it is a marked improvement on what you can see in the previous two images.

Figure 7.3: The same image at 800 × 600 displayed on a screen set at 640 × 480.

Figure 7.4: An image at 16 million colours viewed in Windows Paint on a screen set at 256 colours.

Figure 7.5: The same image in Corel Photo Paint in the same 256 colours gives a better result.

Figure 7.6: Optimise the image at 256 colours and the resulting image will be infinitely better.

Changing colour depth on your display

If you are viewing an image with 256 colours or 65,000 colours or even 16.7 million colours, you will need to view it with the appropriate colour depth on the display. In order to resolve this you will have to change the settings on the video card.

1. Go to My Computer and double click on the icon as shown in Figure 7.7.

Figure 7.7 My Computer.

2. Double click on the Control Panels icon (see Figure 7.8).

Control Panel

Figure 7.8 Control Panels.

3. Double click on Display (see Figure 7.9).

Display

Figure 7.9 Display.

4. Click on the Settings tab (see Figure 7.10).

Select the required colour depth in the Colour Palette menu (see Figure 7.11). 256 colours (8-bit mode) is the minimum requirement for a correct display, 65,000 colours (16-bit) gives a good range of colours, albeit still not vast, and

Figure 7.10 The settings tab in the Display control panel.

Figure 7.11: Select the colour depth you require in the Colour Palette menu.

16.7 million colours (24-bit) more or less covers the whole of the colour spectrum visible to the human eye.

If you can only select 16 or 256 colours at 640 × 480 pixels (see Figure 7.12): either the graphics card is poorly set up (which is the case 99% of the time), or there isn't enough Video RAM on the card (which is fairly unlikely on modern video cards). If the first is true, then go to the next section.

Figure 7.12: You can normally select 16.7 million colours (24-bit mode) at 640 × 480 pixels with a modern video card.

If you have the wrong driver for the card

If you can't display more than 16 or 256 colours at a screen resolution of 640 × 480 pixels or 800 × 600 pixels, it could be that the driver is not the correct one for the video card. The likelihood is that either the driver is not compatible and Windows has chosen another default driver, or that it's an old version that is no longer compatible.

When on installation Windows can't decide the type of the graphics card, it chooses a default which is either Standard graphics card (VGA) or Super VGA. In order to know which it is, click on Change display type.

If you don't have the correct driver, you will have taken a precise course of action.

You know the type of graphics card

In this case, you will know both the make and type of graphics card and which processor it has.

If Windows doesn't autodetect the card correctly, you will have to make sure that you have the latest drivers from the manufacturer of the graphics card at your disposal before you attempt anything further. In the worst case, you could approach the processor manufacturer (Cirrus, Matrox, ATI, S3 and so on) to see if they have drivers which are compatible with the card.

There are two ways you can install the new drivers:

- The card manufacturer might have provided an auto-installer. If this is the case, then all you have to do is insert the disk or CD and follow the instructions.

- The manufacturer has given you the drivers but no installer program. If this is the case, you will have to do the following:

1. In Control Panels, go to Display, Settings and click on Change display settings.

2. Click on the Change button, where it describes the video card.

3. The screen in Figure 7.13 gives us a list of compatible devices. Ignore this and instead click directly on the button that says Have Disk (even if you have a CD).

Figure 7.13 A list of compatible devices ignore it.

4. By now you should be at the same screen as Figure 7.14. If you have the driver on disk, then click OK. If the driver has been supplied on CD-ROM, click on Browse and search through the CD for the driver. In these examples, we have downloaded the driver from the Internet as an EXE file and subsequently copied to the PCTRID directory on the hard drive.

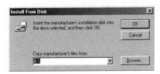

Figure 7.14 Where is the driver?

5. Type in c:\pctrid and click OK. We selected all devices so that the entire list would be available to us. If you know what type of card or processor you have, then select it and click OK.

6. Once you have finished making all the necessary changes, the computer will ask you to restart. If the PC stalls on start up, then it's fairly obvious that the driver is not working. Reboot the PC in safe mode (a menu will be displayed on restarting the PC), and reinstall the standard (VGA) driver you had previously and which is available when you get to the menu in Figure 7.15.

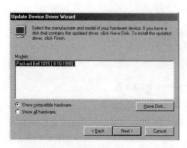

Figure 7.15 The list of all the drivers that was either on the disk or downloaded.

You don't know what type of card it is

If you don't know what type of card you have and don't know which driver to choose, use the detect new hardware function (by selecting Control Panels, Add Device, Auto detect); a device that is already installed under Windows may be preventing the card from being installed. If the problem continues, consult your retailer.

■ Pixels per inch

Sometimes an image may not take up the exact area on screen that it takes up in pixels. For example, an image at 800 × 600 pixels doesn't take up any more than a quarter of your screen, which is also set up to 800 × 600. The problem comes from translating the image size to the screen, these two are measured in ppi (pixels per inch) or dpi (dots per inch) (1 inch = 2.54 cm). A monitor is often defined at 72 and 75 dpi. A scanner may vary between 30 to 600 or 1200 dpi, or more. So for the scanned image to fit the screen it needs to be scanned at 72 or 75 dpi.

Retouching software maintains the resolution set by the scanner after the scanning session. By way of example, Figure 7.16 shows an open file at a resolution of 800 × 542: you can only see a small part of the image, because, for the scanner, the image definition is set at 232 dpi. If you change this to

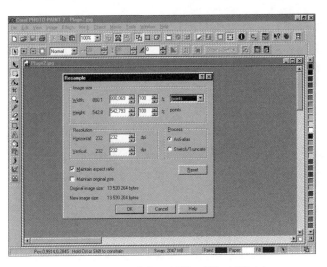

Figure 7.16 An image at a resolution of 800 × 542, at 232 dpi.

72 dpi, you end up with the result in Figure 7.17. You can now see the entire image and you haven't had to alter its physical dimensions.

Although the definition is between 72 and 75 dpi on screen, it's a totally different story on paper when you want to print the job: the resolution of an image for print must be equal to or greater than 300 dpi. If the resolution is not appropriate to the desired printed outcome, then it will look something like Figure 7.18.

Resolution is expressed in pixels per inch. This means the number of pixels used to make up an image in a 2.54 cm (1 inch) segment.

Let's take an image that has been scanned at 72 dpi: it only has 72 pixels for each section of an inch. In order to get magazine quality printing you need to have at least 300 dpi. The ratio between these is therefore 4.16. You can do one of two

Figure 7.17 The same image, at the same resolution, but at 72 dpi.

Figure 7.18 A 72 dpi image printed on paper.

things: either you can decrease the image physical dimension by 4.16 times – which will give you a resolution of 300 dpi but a much smaller image – or you can maintain the image at 100% size (whereby each pixel is artificially enlarged 4.16 times until it fills the required print area; this is what gives the image a ragged and fuzzy appearance as in Figure 7.18).

You should always try and scan images at the resolution at which you intend to use them. 72 dpi is normally only used for screen images and most commonly for the Internet, whereas 300 dpi is used for printing images on paper (in the case of a photo-quality printer, you would use special photographic paper). When you scan at a higher resolution, you are actually increasing the resolution to be able to enlarge the image when printing. For example, if you want to enlarge a 10 × 15 cm photograph to A4, you should scan the original at 600 dpi: it's the only way to maintain the quality of the image when printing at high quality over a full page. To print the same picture at A3, you

will have to scan it at 1200 dpi and so on. Be aware that the higher the resolution you want from the scanner, the longer the scan will take (there are other reasons why scanning takes a while, amongst which are the type and model of the scanner, the way it's connected and the model of the PC).

8 Retouching images

The standard tools palette

Brightness, contrast

Calibration basics

Once you have scanned in the image and you have it in the retouching software, you have endless possibilities for manipulating the image. We will be looking at the main functions in retouching packages that you will use most often.

■ The standard tools palette

A picture is worth a thousand words, so have a look at Figure 8.1, which shows what tools are generally available in retouching packages. We will look at the main characteristics of these tools in the following paragraphs.

Selection tool

Normally used to select an area of the image with which you want to work. If you don't make a selection, all the other tools in the palette will be unavailable.

Marquee		Move
Lasso		Magic Wand
Airbrush		Paintbrush
Rubber Stamp		History Brush
Eraser		Pencil
Blur		Dodge
Pen		Text
Measure		Gradient
Paint Bucket		Eye Dropper
Hand		Zoom

Figure 8.1 Standard Tools palette (in Adobe Photoshop 5.0).

The selection tool can be activated in various ways: you can double click on it, or click and drag whilst holding the mouse button. In Adobe Photoshop, you will see the different selection tools as in Figure 8.2.

Figure 8.2 Different types of selection tool.

Lasso

The lasso is also an image selection tool. Its main purpose is to be able to trace the outline of an object with precision. Adobe Photoshop has three sorts of lasso (see Figure 8.3): free form lasso, polygonal lasso that makes it easier to draw along straight lines and geometric shapes, and the magnetic lasso, which will automatically detect the edge of the image and stick to it (depending on how you set it, it can distinguish between lighter and darker areas and different coloured pixels).

Figure 8.3 Different types of Lasso available in Photoshop.

Airbrush

The airbrush is the artist's preferred tool. It works a little like a paint bomb. The more you concentrate in one area, the more you will cover; if you select a higher throughput, you will get a bigger spray (a little like pressing harder or softer on an aerosol spray). If you move the airbrush quickly over a certain area, you will find that it will be sparsely covered. You will find this function also on some graphics tablets, which are touch and pressure sensitive (Wacom tablets, for example).

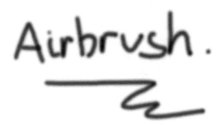

Figure 8.4 An airbrushed example.

Rubber stamp tool

You can use the rubber stamp in one of two modes. You can use it as a rubber stamp to clone areas, which will copy a portion of the image (use the Copy command from the Edit menu) that can then be reproduced anywhere in the image. It can also be used as a pattern stamp. You can use the stamp to create the background of the image, almost as if the stamp is magically making areas of the background appear.

Figure 8.5: The centre of the image is the original that has been rubber stamped.

Figure 8.6: Two working modes for the stamp tool.

Eraser

Used to delete areas of an image, just like the name suggests. You can normally select the size and shape of the eraser so it fits what you need it for. The shape can be either airbrush, pencil, or paintbrush. Or you can use the standard block. As is the case with a large number of tools, you won't be able to use the eraser unless you select the area first.

Blur tool

The blur tool is used to make the same effect on the scanned image that you would make if you dropped some water on a piece of paper: colours would wash out. In Adobe Photoshop, this tool has three settings. The most useful one is the third one, which is called the smudge tool, which lets you spread the colours in a portion of the image, and to blur the edges of an image portion that you want to insert and blend in.

Pen tool

The pen tool lets you draw shapes which can still be edited in terms of size and thickness and so on. It is the best tool to vector draw over shapes that you need for a drawing job. In stark contrast to a bitmap which is made of pixels, vector mode lets you edit a drawn shape by modifying the size and shape of the sections that make it up, all the time maintaining clarity of definition and scalability. This tool, which is in Adobe Photoshop, is rarely available in image manipulation packages, because it is meant to be more for vector drawing packages such as Micrografx Windows Draw, Corel Draw, Adobe Illustrator, Macromedia Freehand and so on.

Figure 8.7: Different types of pen tool available in Adobe Photoshop.

Measure tool

The measure tool lets you see the true size of an image or an area within it. It's not always available on scanning software or retouching software because it is intended more for graphics professionals.

Paint Bucket tool

Absolutely indispensable, you will need the paint bucket to fill a pre-selected area with colour, or a vignette or even a pattern.

Hand tool

You will need the hand tool to be able to navigate the image; if it's too large for the screen, you can just select the tool and scroll the image in any direction. It is also useful if you are working in a magnified view. Double clicking on the hand toll will enlarge the image to fill the screen.

Move tool

The move tool will let you move the image on the screen. You won't always see this tool in other software. In order to achieve this, the software must view each part of the image as separate. For example, if you have put some text into an image, only software that can work in layers will be able to keep these two different items separate, allowing you to move the layers separately. Many low end retouching packages won't let you move items or delete text once you have changed other areas of the image.

 As a cautionary note, even in professional standard software, just saving the image in certain formats will stop you from using it further in other software. If you haven't finished manipulating the image, you will have to save it in native file format so that you can go back to it and work on the separate layers. Corel Photo Paint's native format is shown by the file extension .CPT ; in Photoshop, this is .PSD or .PDD.

Magic wand

This is truly a magic tool that selects an area based on tolerance and by analysing the pixel shadings. In Figure 8.7, the colour reference chosen for automatic analysis was selected

with the eyedropper tool (see section on eyedropper tool).
The higher the shading contrast in pixels, the more precise
the selection will be.

You can also use this tool to replace one colour with another. It will take you seconds to paint a blue car orange.

Figure 8.8: The magic wand is a particularly useful selection tool.

Paintbrush

The paintbrush is common to all image manipulation software. It works just like a real brush: you choose the size and
shape of the brush, and just start painting.

History brush

You will only find this function in high-end software. You
can remove some modifications and rebuild the original
image. It's a little like making your old wallpaper reappear in
its original state, wherever you want.

Pencil tool

Just like the paintbrush, the pencil works exactly like the real item it is modelled on. It lets you draw just as if you were using an HB pencil. The difference between this and the paintbrush is that the pencil tool doesn't draw smudged lines.

Dodge tool

The dodge tool lets you lighten up an area of an image pixel by pixel without altering the content. The tool lets you lighten up shadow areas and subdue unwanted highlights.

Text tool

You will be able to write text and integrate this with your image if you have this tool. Note that some software does not let you modify or move text after having used another function. High-end software lets you change text as often as you like, so long as the file has been saved in native format to maintain the separate elements.

Colour graduation tool

This tool allows you to apply a graduated colour to a pre-selected area. You can make graduations with all sorts of colours. It is, however, better to make graduations (or vignettes) using the same colour and working from a dark tint to a light tint. There are many types of graduation: conical, rectangular, linear, angle and so on.

Figure 8.9: Different graduations in Adobe Photoshop.

Figure 8.10: Graduation tools in the palette.

120

Eyedropper tool

The eyedropper tool is an interesting tool, because it lets you sample a colour directly from the image so that you can use it with the other tools.

Zoom tool

The zoom tool lets you magnify so that you can work close up. This tool can zoom you in to the image so that you can get right to the pixel level.

▪ Brightness, contrast

Brightness and contrast let you change an image which has been scanned when the original is too dark or doesn't have enough definition (if the problem occurs on scanning, then the problem lies in the calibration).

These functions can normally be found in the Edit or Image menus, under Adjust.

▪ Calibration basics

You will no doubt have noticed that the final result often doesn't correspond to the original that you have scanned. This difference is due to a calibration problem chain including the scanner, the screen and the printer. A poor original will not let you get a perfect result but, with a little patience, you can improve the result.

In order to understand the basics of colour calibration, we need to understand that colour monitors do not work in the same colour space as printers. Monitors work in RGB (Red, Green, Blue) whereas a printer works in Cyan, Magenta, Yellow and Black, just to add definition (referred to as Key, hence CMYK). The colours themselves – the four additive

Figure 8.11 The original image is a little dark and does not have enough contrast.

Figure 8.12 The same image after brightness and contrast adjustment.

colours that a printer uses to represent any colour in the visible spectrum – cannot be represented exactly in the same way by a monitor, because the monitor doesn't use the same colour reference. Moreover, a monitor display relies on backlighting (the direction of the light is from the back of the screen) whereas printed paper gets its light externally and displays the colour on the surface. Graphics professionals adjust their monitors every day and even switch them on half an hour before calibration to try and get as perfect a result as possible!

The most sensible way to calibrate a colour chain is to use a colour reference profile, so that a common colour palette is achieved. Some publishers (including Corel) and some scanner manufacturers (including Logitech and Microtek) supply a photograph or reference to allow you to calibrate colour. If you don't have this, you could get a tool of this type from a professional photographer or you could try and make one yourself.

Making a colour reference palette involves making a colour grid in your retouching software. Since you will not be able to trust the screen for colour, you will have to rely on the software definitions of the colours: the software will make the colours according to tint percentages and therefore should be accurate.

As in Figure 8.13, the goal is to create eight rows of little blocks, each row staring with a white block and ending with the pure colour constituent of colour monitors and printers, plus black.

Table 8.1 shows the colours that need to be created as RGB values.

Table 8.1 RGB values to make all the palette colours

Desired colour	Value Red	Value Green	Value Blue
Red	255	0	0
Green	0	255	0
Blue	0	0	255
Cyan	0	255	255
Magenta	255	0	255
Yellow	255	255	0
White	255	255	255
Black	0	0	0

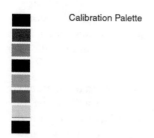

Calibration Palette

Figure 8.13 Reference bar.

To create your own colour reference bar or palette, all you have to do is fill the blocks in the palette with the right colours, based on RGB coding (see Table 8.1). To do this, your software must be able to let you choose the colour mode that you want. By default it will give you RGB instead of other modes. In Figure 8.14, we can see that Photoshop shows the values of the selected colour in all the main colour standards: CMYK, RGB, Lab and HSB.

Figure 8.14 Colours are always translated to values.

Calibrating the printer

To calibrate the printer you must either use the supplied palette or the one you have just made. Use a suitably heavy white paper (100gsm or more). Use all the setting tools you can to change the print area until you can fill the page with Cyan, Magenta and Yellow. Don't bother with Red, Green and Blue. Don't forget to select fine quality in the printer settings. If the printing software asks you what colour model to use, select RGB (see Figure 8.15).

Figure 8.15 Choose RGB colours if you get the choice.

Calibrating the scanner

Calibrating a scanner is a fairly complicated task, and gets even worse if the scanner isn't a particularly good one (you will probably never get it truly calibrated if it isn't any good). Start scanning the palette that you have just printed (or that has been supplied). After this, have a look at the colour make-up of each block. Use the eyedropper for this, starting with the white which should show the values 255, 255 and 255. If you don't get the readings a perfect white should give, even though you have used an ultra-white high-quality paper, rescan the image after placing one or more white sheets on the back of the image to stop the light from shining through the paper (except for sheet fed scanners). If you still don't get a perfect white, then try and resolve the issue by looking at the RGB values that make up the white, after selecting them with the eyedropper. If all the values are out by more or less the same amount, you will have to change the values in the Twain driver (consult the scanner documentation).

If the values show that one of the constituent RGB colours is higher than the other, you will resolve the problem by changing the corresponding colour curve (see Figure 8.16).

Figure 8.16 You can alter colour curves in most good Twain drivers.

Once you have solved the issue with the white, you will then have to go through the RGB of each colour in the palette and adjust the curves accordingly to try and find the best balance. Don't worry about Cyan Magenta and Yellow because these are only used to calibrate the printer.

It should not take longer than an hour to calibrate your scanner, if it is of reasonable quality.

Calibrating the monitor

Colour temperature measured in Kelvin degrees normally governs monitor calibration. A good monitor can be calibrated to a fairly precise colour temperature. If you have good software, you might even be able to calibrate taking into account ambient light and location of the monitor, amongst other factors.

Windows 98 has introduced a new way of making sure everything is calibrated. In Control Panels, select Display, Settings, Advanced: and you will get to the dialog as in Figure 8.17.

Thanks to the Add button, you can add in a list of colour profiles: all you need to do now is choose the one that corresponds to your monitor or the colour handling you are using, for example with the printer (see Figure 8.18).

Figure 8.17 Colour handling, new in Windows 98.

Figure 8.18 Different colour profiles under Windows 98.

9 Case studies

Features of Adobe PhotoDeluxe 2.0

Cutting out an image with Corel PhotoPaint

We will use this chapter to cover actual retouching software and to give examples so as to give you a good idea of what there is around on the market currently. This should be a little more fun than previous lessons! You will also be able to see that different packages often have common features.

■ Features of Adobe PhotoDeluxe 2.0

Adobe PhotoDeluxe 2.0 is often bundled with digital cameras or scanners. It's also available separately, at a good price. This software has all sorts of features, but we will limit ourselves to looking at the basic features which get the most use and let us have the most fun with a few mouse clicks!

Figure 9.1 Load up the image you want to change.

Ageing and daubing

Adobe PhotoDeluxe has a vast selection of filters which can instantly change the look of a picture. In order to use these effects, load up the image and click on the Special Effects button (see Figure 9.1).

First of all you are going to age the image just like it was an old postcard you've found at the bottom of a file in your attic. To achieve this, choose the Age Picture tab.

The first step is to convert from colour to grey: just click on the Color to B&W tab to achieve this (see Figure 9.2).

By clicking on the tints tab, you will get to a whole host of tint colours to age the image. Sepia tint is typical of old photos and is based on a shade of orange. All you have to do to get a sepia tone is to apply a tint of orange to the image.

Figure 9.2 The image is now black and white.

Figure 9.3 Just apply a tint of orange to turn the image into a sepia tone.

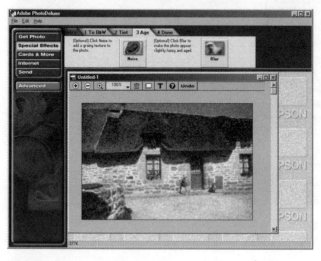

Figure 9.4 If you want to take the effect to the limit, select ageing and noise to give the surface a cracked effect.

The third tab lets you apply a cracked surface effect to the image, by clicking on the Noise button (see Figure 9.4).

If you didn't want to make the picture look old but just wanted to make it look like a painting, all you would have to do is select Special Effects, click on the Impressionist button and choose the Crystallize option to get to the effect in Figure 9.5 within a few seconds.

Figure 9.5 The Impressionist effect turns the image into a painting in seconds.

Correcting the colour balance

PhotoDeluxe has an excellent automatically correct colour balance. The example in Figure 9.6 is very clear: the original on the slide is of a good quality, but the scanned image is very dark and with poor contrast.

Select Photo, Aspect, Autolevels in order to rebalance the colours (see Figure 9.7). After this is done, it is possible to

Figure 9.6 Before autolevels.

Figure 9.7 After autolevels, the contrast is much better and so is the colour.

change the brightness and contrast manually to get a better result.

Selection simplified

Adobe PhotoDeluxe simplifies selecting an area thanks to its Optimised Selection tool (see Figure 9.8).

This semi-automatic function helps you to easily cut out pictures. You choose the starting point and then follow the line you need to cut out. The program tries to help by following the line that you are tracing. This is how you can cut out images which have good contrasting areas in minutes rather than in hours if you were to do this 100% manually.

Figure 9.8 The optimised selection function makes it so much easier to make cut-outs.

Montage cut-outs on backgrounds

PhotoDeluxe 2.0 lets you montage cut-outs of people or objects on to predefined backgrounds. Figure 9.9 shows a clipart library for people who don't have a scanner or can't get images electronically, for example by e-mail.

Figure 9.9 A clipart library.

Let's take the basketball player as an example; you can cut it out thanks to the Autoselect tool, then copy it to the pasteboard, close the original, then open the Eiffel Tower image which is also in the clipart library and paste the basketball player into it, resizing the basketball player as required. In less than 10 minutes you should be looking at something similar to Figure 9.10. Of course, there is more that you can do to it to refine the image, but this is the process to achieve something almost completely automatically.

Calendars, greetings cards and so on

PhotoDeluxe also has lots of templated functions to create calendars, business cards, greetings cards and so on. Doing this is simple: once you have finished retouching the image you

Figure 9.10 It took just 10 minutes to montage this basket ball player onto the Eiffel tower.

want, all you have to do is click on the button that says Cards and so on to get to the menu that contains all the different types of products. You can choose Calendar, for example, and save it with a name. This is now included in the clipart library on the side. All you have to do at this point is select the type of calendar, the way it looks and the font, then all that is left to do is drag and drop from the clipart library to the calendar and resize the images accordingly. You will then end up with something like Figure 9.11.

Export formats

PhotoDeluxe is a feature- and resource-rich program, which is also very flexible in terms of saving into various formats. You can also use Adobe's famous PDF format, which you will find in the File menu, Export, Acrobat PDF file. This format is particularly useful because it is universal and keeps layouts

Figure 9.11 A personalised calendar in Adobe PhotoDeluxe.

and print quality exactly the same as the original document, whatever the computer that the document is displayed on (Macintosh or PC). The only tip to fully take advantage of font quality in the document creation is to install all the PhotoDeluxe options from the beginning, including ATM and all the fonts that come with it. PhotoDeluxe also saves Internet compatible file formats (GIF, JPEG), BMP format which is native to Windows and Paint (which also lets you make desktop wallpaper) and screen saver format. This last format lets you attach one image after another to create a series for a screen saver.

■ Cutting out an image with Corel PhotoPaint

Photomontage is fun, letting you put together people who have never met, or put people in a situation they have never been in or in a place they have never lived, or, at its simplest, make a picture prettier. Some postcard publishers wouldn't hesitate to take a mountain top and move it just to make a place more attractive! We will show you how to cut out objects so that you can then montage them in another image.

Preparing the scan of the object or person to cut out

Before attempting a cut-out, you must be aware that this operation requires patience and a steady hand. First of all, the image must be scanned in at sufficient resolution. For our demonstration we have chosen to scan a 35mm transparency at 1000 dpi (which is the smallest size to scan at, considering the size of a 35mm transparency) with a Microtek ScanMaker 35t Plus, which is a good scanner for those who prefer to work with transparencies rather than reflective originals. Another good point about this scanner is that it can scan colour negatives and black and whites. Start by doing a prescan (a function which lets you scan in a representation for you to make your selection before scanning at high resolution; you can accurately select the part of the image you need). In our example, we have chosen to cut out the car; so we will start by selecting an area as close to the car as possible (see Figure 9.12).

Scanning parameters have been set at 1000dpi. Since this particular scanner can reach 1900dpi in optical resolution (true resolution) and 3900dpi interpolated scanning mode that simulates a higher resolution than the scanner truly has, we would have been able to scan at a higher resolution if we needed to create a photomontage for the centre spread of a magazine. Once we have changed the settings, let's start scanning: Corel Photo Paint displays the image directly on your screen (see Figure 9.13).

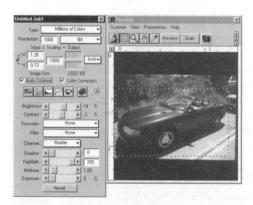

Figure 9.12 After the prescan, you must select an area as close to the finished item as you can.

Figure 9.13 The image is displayed at the scanned size and resolution.

Zoom mode

Once the image has been loaded, select Zoom mode by clicking on the magnifying glass on the tool bar and select the area that you need to work with. You must be really close up to get the cut-out accurate, almost down to pixel level. Figure 9.14 shows the displayed image at a size where we could start to do the cut-out.

Figure 9.14 You can start to see the cut-out at this level of magnification.

When you double click on the paintbrush you get the dialog box as in Figure 9.15.

You will have to choose a brush size that will let you trace the outline of the cut-out accurately. In the selected zoom mode, we have selected a 5-pixel diameter brush. At this stage, this is accurate enough to make a good cut-out (see Figure 9.16).

If you make a mistake, don't forget that Corel Photo Paint has an Undo function which lets you go back over the last operation, but there is also an Undo List (in the Edit menu) which lets you go back a few steps (see Figure 9.17).

Figure 9.15 The brush tool dialog box.

Figure 9.16 Start cutting out, keep reviewing the accuracy of the brush and change it if necessary.

Figure 9.17 The Undo list lets you go back and retrace your steps.

To draw around straight objects, always try and use the Polygon tool. This tool is selected by clicking on the side bar, and, holding down the mouse button, moving the mouse towards the triangular icon (see Figure 9.18).

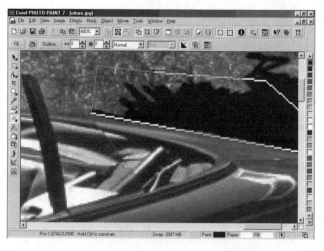

Figure 9.18 The Polygon tool is particularly useful for drawing in straight lines.

Make sure you OK the tool away from where you have just drawn, so that a diagonal line doesn't get drawn and exclude part of the drawing you wanted (see Figure 9.19).

Once you have finished tracing the outline (see Figure 9.20), delete what you don't need by using the Rectangle Selection tool.

Notice that in Figure 9.21, the cut-out is nearly perfect.

Figure 9.19 Always OK the tool away from the area you have just selected

Figure 9.20 The cut-out is nearly finished.

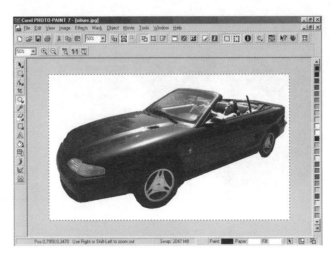

Figure 9.21 All that's left is the car.

Finishing touches

Several details on the picture do not look right: straight lines, almost square wheels. There are plenty of tools available to make changes to the picture, amongst which the Cotton bud, which lets you blend colours. In the example in Figure 9.22, we have used the Cotton bud to round off the wheels and the body lines of the car – not a quick job at all.

Once you have an acceptable image, simply paste it into another image. In Figure 9.23 we have scanned an image of a beach.

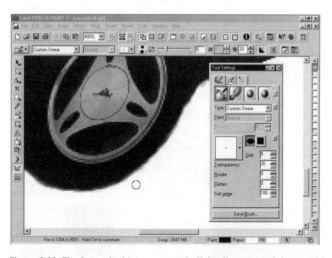

Figure 9.22 The Cotton bud lets you round off details you aren't happy with.

Figure 9.23 A beach.

Creating a mask and montageing it

Since the car is completely cut out, it will be easy to make a mask (same principle as a stencil in painting) letting us combine it with the beach image. Select Mask, Color Mask: and the dialog in Figure 9.24 will appear.

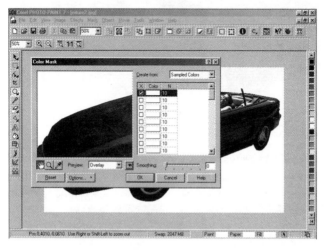

Figure 9.24 Dialog for creating a mask.

Using the hand tool in the Review area, move the image around until you have seen the whole picture that has been cut out.

Select the eyedropper and click on the cut-out colour: in this instance, it is white.

In the dialog box, the first colour in the area on the right should be selected. Click OK: and the object will be surrounded with points (see Figure 9.25).

Figure 9.25 The car is surrounded with points.

You can now use the Copy and Paste commands in Corel PhotoPaint. Go to the other image you opened (the beach) and select Paste As New Object in the Edit menu. The result will be as Figure 9.26.

All you need to do now is move the car to wherever you want it and reduce or enlarge it as you wish, to make it fit the perspective of the picture. Once you have finished, you should flatten the image to the background: for this you need to select Combine under the object menu and go to the Objects with Background option (see Figure 9.27).

And the finished item is in Figure 9.28.

All that is left at this stage is to add the realistic touches by sinking the wheels in the sand, taking out the jaggies and so on. Figure 9.29 shows the image that has been worked on a little more and has been reframed: the image is not perfect, but it is quite convincing.

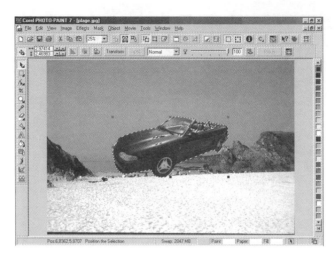

Figure 9.26 The car has been pasted into the background.

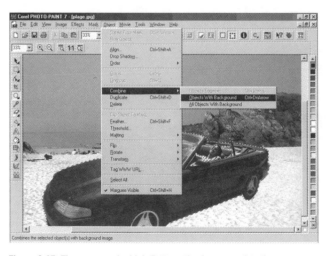

Figure 9.27 The command which flattens the foreground to the
background.

Figure 9.28 The finished montage with all images flattened.

Figure 9.29 Almost had me fooled...

10
Saving images for the Internet

JPEG for colours

GIF, completely transparent

Creating images with transparency

Making an animated GIF

Internet bandwidth isn't very high. Your modem probably doesn't help much, since, even in optimum conditions, a 56KBps modem is only capable of downloading 400KB of information a minute, at best. The smallest image made with Paint will be about 400KB, or even 1 or 2 MB. So the Paint format is obviously not going to help net surfers go from site to site and view images with any degree of speed! In practice there are two formats that dominate the Web world: JPEG and GIF.

■ JPEG for colours

JPEG images can generally be recognised as such by their file extension: .JPG. It is a compressed file format that includes 16.7 million colours which is the entire spectrum visible to the human eye. The format is completely cross platform now, whereas some years ago it was necessary to install a special card to be able to compress JPEG formats in very little time.

Currently, a Pentium would only take a few seconds to resample an image from 1MB to 100KB or even 50KB, all the while maintaining the quality aspect. Figure 10.1 shows the difference between the full blown image and the compressed image: the image on the left is uncompressed at 3MB, whereas the one on the right is JPEG compressed to 400KB by a factor of 40. Figure 10.2 shows the visual difference between the two images.

Certainly there are differences, but would we have noticed without the original being there? For all this, we can't use this compression ratio for printed matter (apart from, maybe in a catalogue with very small images). Moreover, the JPEG format has an inconvenient side: it can't be used in transparency.

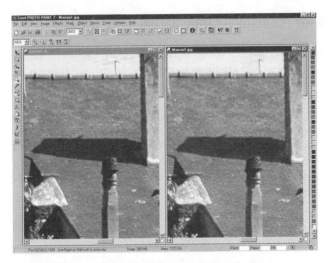

Figure 10.1 On the left, the original; on the right, the JPEG image compressed by a factor of 40.

Figure 10.2 Images seen in perspective.

■ GIF, completely transparent

In the GIF format, which was invented by CompuServe, the compression is based on the number of colours rather than on the fineness of the image. The GIF format only allows for 256 colours maximum. Often, this colour depletion is invisible to the naked eye. As a starting point, a GIF format image takes up more space than a JPEG (up to twice as much), but is much more accurate. Moreover the GIF format allows you to use any colour of the palette as a transparent colour. Figure 10.3 shows the same image saved as a JPEG and a GIF with transparency set on black. This transparent GIF is called Gif 89a.

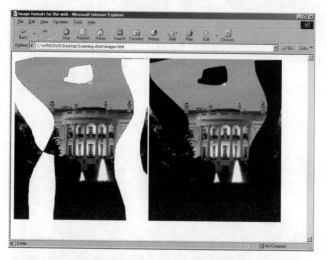

Figure 10.3 On the left, a GIF with transparency on black; on the right, the same image with JPEG compression.

■ Creating images with transparency

Images on the Web are not necessarily a rectangle: they can be all shapes and sizes. Quite often the image looks as though it has been cut out. This is due to using the Gif 89a format with transparency colour. It is this transparent colour that separates the image from its bounding box, that gives the impression that the image has a specific shape. Note that JPEGs don't allow for this sort of treatment.

Starting point

If you have a good package such as PaintShop Pro, Photoshop, Corel PhotoPaint or some other software that is able to save in GIF format, launch it. For best results, start with an image at 16.7 million colours, no matter what the format (BMP, JPEG, TIF and so on) rather than with an image with 256 colours. If you do use a 256 colour image, you will be risking using one of its important colours for the transparency, which will make parts of the image transparent that you don't want to (see Figure 10.4)!

Figure 10.4 Typical example starting from a 256 colour image.

Making a cut-out

To make a cut-out you have to use a vivid colour to define the area on the picture. Avoid black and white, as these are often in images to a greater or lesser degree. Try and use either magenta or a very bright yellow. Once you have chosen the colour you want, you can use all the tools you need in the palette apart from ones that create anti-aliasing: the bounds of the image must be sharp and well defined (see Figure 10.5).

To get a perfect background, don't hesitate to use the polygon tool by filling it with the same colour as the outline. It's certainly one of the most efficient tools to make a cut-out (see Figure 10.6). Once the cut-out has been made, make sure that the transparent part of the image is completely uniform, right up to the bounding box: even the slightest imperfection will show up.

Figure 10.5 Cut the image out with a brush and a vivid colour.

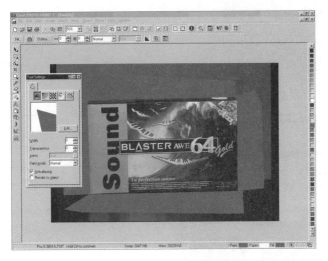

Figure 10.6 To mark the area better, fill the polygon selection.

Converting to 256 colours

You will now have to decrease the number of colours used in the image from 16.7 million colours to 65,000 to 256 colours. If your software is of a reasonable standard, this should not pose any problem. If you are using Corel PhotoPaint, select Image, then Convert To, Paletted (8-bit). The choice you are presented with (see Figure 10.7) tells you that you can convert to 256 colours optimised: you should click OK.

The image displayed will be pretty close to the original. The difference lies in the palette they use. As you can see from Figure 10.8, the two palettes are very different indeed. Note, however, how the colour we chose for the cut-out background is the same.

Figure 10.7 Always select optimised 8-bit format.

Figure 10.8 16.7 million colours vs. 256 colours – the colour we chose for the cut-out is the same in both palettes.

Saving in Gif 89a

If you simply want to convert an image, all you need to do is to save the image in standard GIF format without any special settings. In order to benefit from a transparency, you would have to save it with transparency included. Then choose the colour that you want as transparent (see Figure 10.9).

Then OK and save. In Figure 10.10, we have juxtaposed two GIF version images: the standard version is on the left and the transparent version is on the right. The difference is pretty obvious!

Figure 10.9 You can choose the transparency colour when saving a GIF.

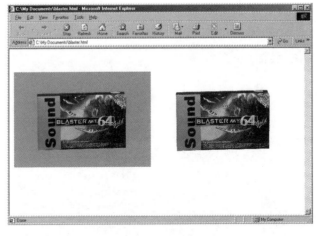

Figure 10.10 The same image saved with and without transparency.

■ Making an animated GIF

Just like any video or film, an animated GIF is made up of frames which are run one after the other. You must use good software and plan the animation prior to embarking on creating one, so that it won't be too big to download. To show you that an animated GIF can be worked on forever, we have picked different software to make up all the parts.

Definition of frames

Creating an animated sequence starts with characters, all coming from image retouching software. As a starting point (see Figure 10.11), we have chosen a completely new banner with the word 'edito'.

In order to make the 'edito' button a central character in the banner, we have to start with placing it on the banner (see Figure 10.12).

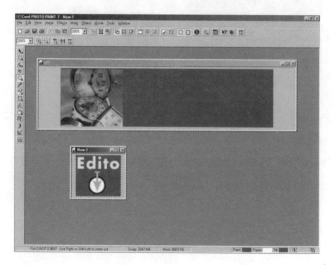

Figure 10.11 The characters, the banner, and the 'edito' button.

Figure 10.12 The character is pasted in for the first time.

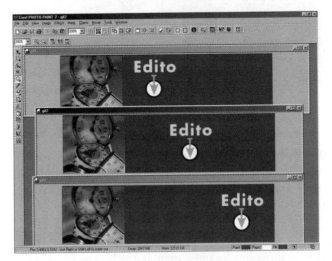

Figure 10.13 The three files that will be used to create an animation.

We then saved this as the first GIF file, as gif1.gif. Our aim is to create three files where the word 'edito' will appear in a different place on all occasions (see Figure 10.13).

Corel PhotoPaint lets you make animated GIFS but we have decided to use Gif Movie Gear, which is an excellent piece of free software available from **http://www.shareware.com**.

Making the animation

In Gif Movie Gear, all you have to do is use the Insert Frame command in the File menu. As you can see from Figure 10.14, the process doesn't present any difficulties.

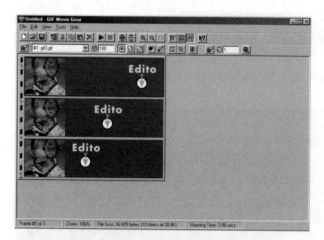

Figure 10.14 The three files have been inserted as frames.

If you want a preview of the GIF, then just click Play (see Figure 10.15).

If you are happy with the result, save the animation. In our example, the banner is 36KB, even with the image being made of three smaller ones, each at 13KB, which represents pretty poor optimisation. If a surfer wanted to download this image, it would take at least 8 seconds, even if everything was OK. It is true to say that at at this point it is 357 × 150 pixels.

Figure 10.15 Preview in Gif Movie Gear.

Optimising the animation

In Gif Movie Gear, there is an optimisation function. You should get to this and the dialog box (see Figure 10.16 to see how to optimise the animation).

The good point about the menu: it tells you exactly what the savings are by doing what you are doing. As you can see, it's fairly easy to make it so a surfer only has a few items to download. You can see that optimisation is illustrated in Figure 10.17: the software suppresses what isn't used.

Another reason to use Gif Movie Gear is to reduce the number of colours from 256 to 128, 64, 32 or 16, as long as it fits the speed you want to run at. In our example, we have changed the colour depth to 16 colours This accident has shown us how the software functions and has given them extra when they need it most.

This has also meant that this method of compression has allowed us to go from 36KB to 7KB. So now we will be spending about one second downloading the stuff instead of the eight seconds we had before.

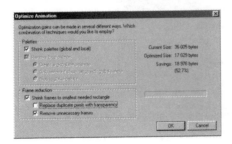

Figure 10.16 The GIF optimisation process

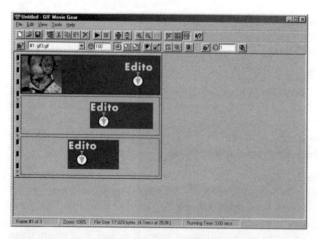

Figure 10.17 Many superfluous pixels have been removed by the software.

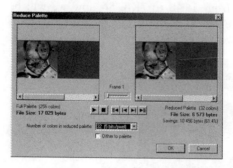

Figure 10.18 Colour resampling and subsequent time reaction.

11
Internet photos by e-mail

■ ■ ■ ■ ■ ■ ■ ■ ■ ■ ■ ■ ■ ■ ■ ■ ■ ■ ■

Sending pictures by e-mail

Downloading pictures by e-mail

E-mail addresses without an
Internet subscription

If you are not familiar with Windows
and the Web

If you have the Internet icon on your desktop

If you do not have the Internet icon on
your desktop

■ Sending pictures by e-mail

Sending a picture by e-mail is very straightforward if you have e-mail software: just type in your correspondent's e-mail address (this is the usual format: name@provider.xxx) then include an image file by using the attach function. Let's use Microsoft Internet Mail and Outlook Express as examples (see Figure 11.1), since these are bundled for free with Microsoft Internet Explorer 3.0 and 4.0 respectively: they let you attach an image by using the paper click icon. Once you have clicked on the paper clip, all you have to do is insert the name of the file in the displayed dialog box. You can attach more than one item at a time, but don't exceed 1.5MB (many Internet providers actually limit the mail size to this). If you want to send a larger e-mail, then split it down and send it in batches of several e-mails. Outlook Express (and other e-mail software) lets you view your Inbox and preview images.

Figure 11.1 Sending pictures by e-mail.

■ Downloading pictures by e-mail

Who hasn't ever wished that they could get pictures on to the PC without having to scan them? **www.quicksnaps.co.uk** lets you do exactly that, and is very simple to use. All you have to do is e-mail the images to yourself, and you will then see them in your Inbox. Only one format is usually available: JPEG, normally at a resolution of 800×600 pixels, and with a compression ratio appropriate to the quality of the photo required. The service also accepts prints at 10×15 cm as well as transparencies at 24×36 or negatives, which are very convenient, above all when the prints have deteriorated or yellowed with age. If you don't have an e-mail account, you can get one from subscription services such as Demon.

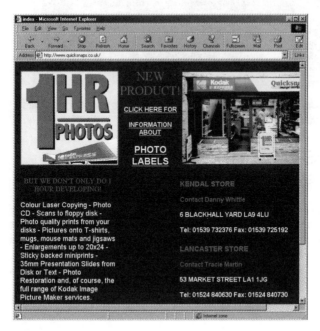

Figure 11.2: www.quicksnaps.co.uk scans your pictures and sends them to your e-mail address.

Figure 11.3 At www.quicksnaps.co.uk you can also have your old photos restored and sent back to you in digital format.

■ E-mail addresses without an Internet subscription

There used to be a time when the Internet was very expensive to use. Not only did you have to pay the bill for the phone call, you also had to pay your ISP a basic rate for service and then another rate for the amount of time you spent on the Internet. However, things are now very different. Most ISPs still charge for service (usually between £5 and £15 a month), but there are also those that offer the service for free. These free service providers fall into two categories. Those who need an established connection to the Internet and those who don't. The former might sound slightly misleading, because in fact you do not actually need to own a computer to be able to use their services. All you need is access to a computer that already has both a connection to the Internet (which is not a difficult task to achieve) and a Java compatible Web browser (such as Internet Explorer 4+, Navigator 3+ and HotJava). Access to the Internet can be found in many places, ranging from Internet cafés to libraries and many educational establishments. Once you have access to the Internet through one of these establishments, all you do is point your Web browser to a relevant site (Figure 11.4) and you will be guided through an easy sign-up process. Possibly one of the best things to do is to go to a search engine such as Yahoo! (**www.yahoo.co.uk**) and type in `free e-mail`. You will then be given a long list of providers to choose from.

Once you have signed up, you can check your e-mail from any Web browser you choose. No extra software is needed. However, with many free providers, technical support is poor, so unless you know what you are doing you might not be able to take full advantage of the services offered by the provider.

The second method requires you to own a computer and a modem, and therefore is not as flexible or mobile as the former method. You can only use the services from that single computer. However, the services and technical support provided are usually of a high standard. One of the more popular free ISPs of this type is Freeserve from the Dixon group. They were one of the early pioneers of free Internet services and Freeserve is now going from strength to strength. Joining is also easy: all you need to do is get an installation CD, which can be found at most shops or magazines (for free). These shops include Dixons, Currys, or even some supermarkets. Once you have your CD, you're ready to join.

Figure 11.4 Some of the available free e-mail service providers in the UK and Ireland.

 Before you undertake any installation or change any settings always have your system disks or CD handy.

Before you start make sure there are no programs open and then insert the Freeserve CD into your drive. The CD will autostart and you will be shown the screen in Figure 11.5. Click on Install…

…You will then be asked to install Internet Explorer 4. You cannot carry on unless you do this, even if you already have it installed. Follow the on-screen instructions and keep all the settings it suggests.

Figure 11.5 Installing Freeserve software.

Figure 11.6 Installing Internet Explorer 4.0.

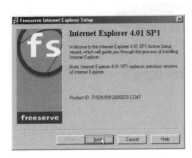

Figure 11.7 Follow the on-screen instructions and keep all settings.

When Internet Explorer setup has finished, your computer will restart. Once this has happened you will be shown the screen in Figure 11.8. If this doesn't happen, then open Internet Explorer (from the Start menu) and the screen will come up automatically.

Click on Continue and the program will attempt to dial the ISP. If this fails, then the phone number may be wrong. In this case, use: 0845–079 6699. You will then be shown the screen in Figure 11.10. Select the new account option. Now you will be asked to provide your personal details, your preferred account name and a password to access your account.

Everything is complete and you are now a member. Every time you start Internet Explorer, it will automatically connect to Freeserve. Now you need to set up your e-mail. This can be done with the help of many mail programs that are available on the market. However, the example used here is Outlook Express, which comes with Internet Explorer. The first thing you need to do is make sure this is your default mail client for Internet explorer (this is useful when browsing the Internet). Open Internet Explorer and stop it from

Figure 11.8 The Freeserve Internet setup.

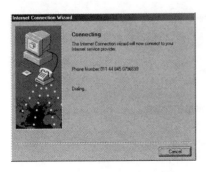

Figure 11.9 The program dials your ISP.

Figure 11.10 Choose the new account option.

connecting by pressing Cancel on the dialling box that appears. Now choose Tools/Internet options.

Click on the Programs tab of the dialog box. On the e-mail drop-down list, choose Outlook Express as the e-mail program (see Figure 11.12). Now click on OK and close Internet Explorer.

Run Outlook Express from the Start menu (see Figure 11.13).

Figure 11.11 Choose Tools, Internet Options.

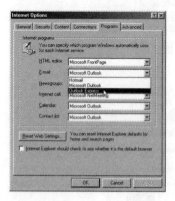

Figure 11.12 Choose Outlook Express as the mail program that is used by Internet Explorer.

The Internet Connection Wizard should start up (Figure 11.14). Type in your name and press Next.

You will then be prompted to give an Internet address. Outlook should have already detected your Freeserve address. If not then enter it.

Check the addresses of the incoming and outgoing mail servers as shown in Figure 11.16 and then click Next. Confirm your username and password, click Next and then finish by clicking on Close. The accounts dialog box will then appear, showing you your account details. From now on, whenever you need to add or remove e-mail accounts that you may have, you will do it from here. This dialog box can be found in the Tools, Accounts menu. Simply click Add and then repeat the process. You can also add news accounts from here. Press Close and you will be taken back to the main program.

Figure 11.13 Running Outlook Express.

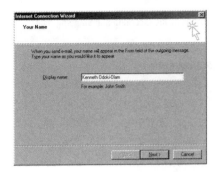

Figure 11.14 The Internet connection Wizard.

Figure 11.15 Type in your Freeserve Address.

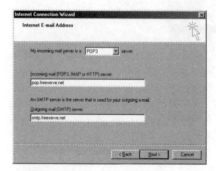

Figure 11.16 Checking the settings of the incoming and outgoing mail servers.

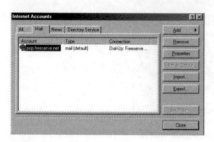

Figure 11.17 The accounts dialog box.

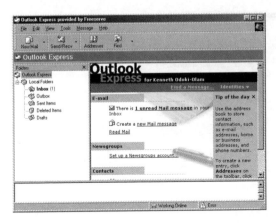

Figure 11.18 The main program.

■ If you are not familiar with Windows and the Web

This section is meant for those who are not familiar with Windows and therefore may well make mistakes when trying to configure their computer for the Web. Procedures are quite simple for Freeserve, as you have seen, but may be slightly more complex for other providers.

■ If you have the Internet icon on your desktop

If you have never used this function.

Double-click on the icon. You will see the menu as in Figure 11.20.

Confirm with the OK button. Then follow the instruction for connecting to Freeserve or to your chosen ISP. They should be able to provide documentation on how to connect to their server (settings usually vary from one ISP to another).

Figure 11.19 This is the dialog that opens when you double-click the Internet icon on your desktop.

Figure 11.20 The first access menu to the configuration in Windows 95.

■ If you do not have the Internet icon on your desktop

You need Windows 95 Dial-Up Networking.

To check that Windows 95 Dial-Up Networking is installed, click on My Computer in your desktop: the Dial-Up Networking icon should be visible (see Figure 11.21).

Windows 95 Dial-Up Networking is installed: check that it is properly configured.

Figure 11.21 The Dial-Up Networking icon in Windows 95.

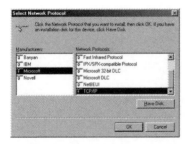

Figure 11.22 When you select Microsoft, the TCP/IP choice is proposed.

If the function is installed, check that the TCP/IP network layer is installed. To do this, go to Control Panel in My Computer, and double-click on the Network icon.

If your PC is not linked to a physical network and Dial-Up Networking is installed, you need to obtain a number of data.

If you do not see any mention of TCP/IP, click on Add. Choose Protocol. Click on Add. Then choose Microsoft and TCP/IP.

179

Confirm by clicking on OK: the files from the diskette or the CD will now be copied. If the TCP/IP layer was not installed previously, the procedure will include restarting your computer.

You can now use the connection procedure described in this chapter.

12 A few last details

■ ■ ■ ■ ■ ■ ■ ■ ■ ■ ■ ■ ■ ■ ■ ■ ■ ■

Printing

Software and advanced functions overview

Photo-CDs

If you wish to print your masterpiece, or to take your creative possibilities a bit further, then this chapter is for you.

■ Printing

The arrival of colour inkjet printers on the market has hugely increased the range of documents that can be printed from a computer. Paper manufacturers have adjusted quickly to this evolution and have been providing fairly exciting new quality paper.

Various printing media

It has always been possible to print documents on various types of paper, namely special photographic paper, indicated for scanned and retouched images, but there is also a number of different types of printing media. The Avery brand offers, for example, special size paper for printing business cards, greeting cards, invites, sticky labels, round or square, CD-ROM labels and so on (this is indeed very interesting for users who wish to create low-cost short runs for their CD-ROM). On the other hand, all printer manufacturers recommend different paper formats, with special media for producing t-shirts! The technique is quite simple: you just print the pattern as mirrored (using the 'mirror' function available in the Edit menu in all retouching software) and then cut out the pattern on the sheet. All you need now is to go over it with a hot iron to press the pattern on the t-shirt. The pattern will stick quite easily, even though colours may fade away, just like any other printed t-shirt.

Printing your work

To be able to print, you need to establish the settings for your printer driver. Obviously, you must have your printer driver installed on your computer.

Figure 12.1 Avery offers various printing media and even provides the relevant software for using them.

Installing your printer driver

Usually, printer manufacturers will provide the installation program for their printer on diskette or CD-ROM. To install the program, refer back to the method shown in Chapter 3, for programs provided with your scanner. You should also refer to the documentation which comes with your printer.

Printing

The procedure for printing is always the same, regardless of the retouching software used:

1. Go to File, Print.
2. A menu is displayed (see Figure 12.2).
3. Check that, in the Printer area, the displayed name corresponds to the printer you wish to print to (if you have several printers installed on your PC).

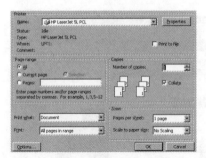

Figure 12.2 The Print menu in Windows.

4. If the name shown is not the name of your printer, click on the arrow to the right of the suggested name and select the name of the printer you wish to use.

5. Confirm with OK.

Modifying the printing options

If you wish to modify the printing options for your printer, do the following:

Figure 12.3 Setting options for your Printer (in this case, a Deskjet 720 C by Hewlett Packard).

1. If the name displayed in the Name box in the dialog box shown in Figure 12.2 is the name of your printer, click on the Properties button.
2. You will now see the setting options for your printer (see Figure 12.3).

You can now choose various print modes: refer to Table 12.1 for a better understanding of the settings and their functions.

Table 12.1 The main setting options and their function

Setting	Function
Paper size	Selects the size of paper that is currently in the printer
Paper type	It is usually sufficient to specify the type of paper actually to be used. But, with some printer drivers, this setting affects print quality. Consequently, often the print quality for 'normal' paper is better than for 'photo paper'. It all depends on the printer: test yours to check whether this is true or not.
Print quality	This works differently for various types of printers. This affects printing speed considerably: in 'draft' quality, printing is clearly faster than in 'best'. The actual printing quality is not only affected by these settings, but also by the choice made for type of paper (including if you trick your printer into error by not specifying the type of paper you are actually going to use).

Setting	Function
Resolution	Some printer drivers will prompt you to specify a printing resolution. The higher the resolution, the better the outcome.
Color	This setting allows you to choose whether you are printing in colour or in black and white
Fineprint/Photograde	This parameter is used for printing graphics and photographs. It affects the printing quality. If you do not print in Fineprint/Photograde, you will obtain a mediocre quality for photos and graphics. The higher the grade, the better the printed outcome.
Orientation	This setting concerns the orientation for the paper in the printer. In Landscape, the paper is printed horizontally. In Portrait, the paper is printed vertically (this is how you would normally print text on A4 paper).
Recto/Verso	This mode is rarely used with photo retouching software. Word processing or typesetting applications use it more often. It allows automatically to define, to the left or to the right, a wider margin which allows you to paginate a bound document or sheets to be included into a folder, with a better visual impact.

■ Software and advanced functions overview

Retouching images, organising one's photo albums, drawing caricatures, publishing on the Web, creating 3D images, designing: these are all activities which have been made possible by a variety of new software packages. These are some examples.

Photo retouching and design software

There is a vast choice for photo retouching and design software. On one hand, there are shareware programs (the best known and most powerful one is Paint Shop Pro), and, on the other hand, there are the commercial programs such as Adobe Photoshop, Corel PhotoPaint and so on. Each of these products offers a large range of options for filters, surface treatment, textures, etc. The most professional program, which has become the benchmark, is Adobe Photoshop. Very expensive, this product is for print and graphic artists working at professional level. As far as you are concerned, you need to choose the program which is best suited to your requirements, in view of what you wish to achieve.

Do-it-yourself photo retouching

The market grows day by day, and it caters more and more for the general public. It is therefore easier nowadays to find products which suit every pocket. The leaders in this market are Adobe PhotoDeluxe 2.0, U-Lead iPhoto Express and Microsoft Picture-It. Metatools, which specialise in special graphic effects, have launched, with Kai's Photo Soap, the simplest and most user-friendly tool one could possibly imagine. With these products, the whole family can truly have a lot of fun with the electronic brush.

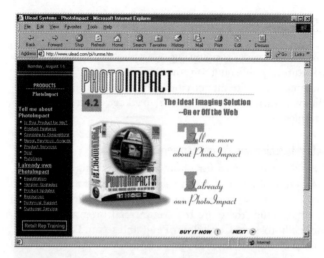

Figure 12.4 PhotoImpact, a retouching software which is simple, high performance and relatively inexpensive.

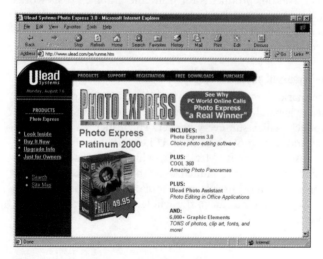

Figure 12.5 iPhotoExpress, a retouching software for family use.

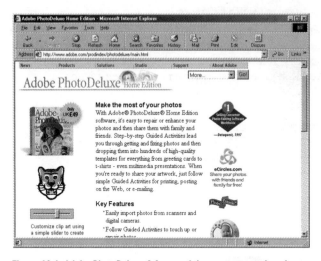

Figure 12.6 Adobe PhotoDeluxe 2.0, one of the most comprehensive tools to create cards, calendars and so on.

Figure 12.7 Kai's Photo Soap, impossible to make it any simpler!

Do-it-yourself with a difference

For those who love caricatures, Metatools has devised Kai's
SuperGoo, a retouching and caricature program which
includes accessories for hair, hats, spectacles, etc. In short,
everything for a pleasant evening between friends…

Figure 12.8 SuperGoo, caricature for fun.

3D tools

The 3D tools family includes various types of programs.
There are some which, such as Live Picture Photo Vista, offer
the possibility of creating landscape views at 360 degrees.
This allows you to 'pivot' with the impression of remaining
at the centre of the picture – with the purpose of presenting
these panoramic views on the Internet or on multimedia
CD-ROMs. There are also programs, such as U-Lead
Cool 3D, which allow you to create logos and fixed or ani-

mated titles using all sorts of textures. And finally there are also programs, such as TrueSpace and Bryce, which allow you to create objects and landscapes, and produce video clips or still images viewed from different angles. You can then play the role of the scriptwriter, designer, cameraman and photographer. The textures applied to the various image elements can also be taken from personal photographs which have been scanned.

Tools for publishing on the Web

There are two programs which share the market for Internet publishing, with retouching options: Adobe PageMill, supplied with a reduced version of Adobe Photoshop, and FrontPage 98 – and now, FrontPage 2000, of course, supplied with Office 2000. These two products, very comprehensive and user-friendly, also allow users to create both personal Web pages and truly professional websites. In both cases, productivity is the name of the game.

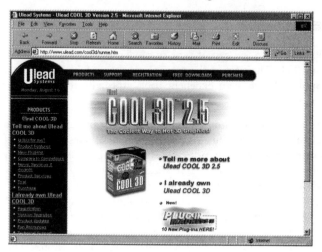

Figure 12.9 Cool 3D offers high-performance tools to create 3D illustrations.

Figure 12.10 Adobe PageMill allows users to create attractive Web pages.

■ Photo-CDs

Photo-CDs are a recent type of media, developed by Kodak in 1991. They are still not very much used by the general public. But it is an excellent tool, especially if you do not have a scanner!

You can use the photos in your Photo-CD on any PC with a CD-ROM compatible Photo-CD (which applies to 99 % of current readers). The principle is very simple: just go to your photo lab, give them your slides or your negatives. After about a week, the lab will provide you with CDs with excellent prints. You can also view your photos on your computer screen, and produce fairly good quality prints (if your printer is up to it). This will cost you some £10 for the blank CD, plus £4.50 per photo (with a minimum run of 20 photos. This information on prices is only indicative and obviously bound to vary from place to place; you should therefore consult your local photo lab, or better still, a number of photo labs, to compare prices). As well as an appropriate CD-ROM reader, to read a Photo-CD your PC needs a program which can read stock photos. The more advanced design and retouching packages integrate this function (but not the less sophisticated ones, such as Windows Paint). Programs published by Corel, Adobe, U-Lead and other publishers will allow you to work with Photo-CD images. Figure 12.11 shows the display of a Photo-CD in Adobe PhotoDeluxe 2.0.

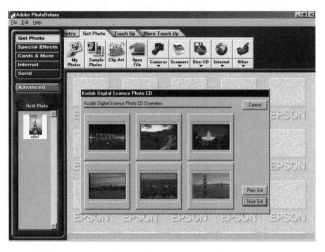

Figure 12.11 With Adobe PhotoDeluxe, reading a Photo-CD is simple and user-friendly.

A
Scanners currently on the market and their features

■ ■

Umax – Astra 1220S
Hewlett Packard – ScanJet 6200C
Canon – CanoScan FB 620
Umax – PowerLook III
Agfa – SnapScan
Hewlett Packard – ScanJet 4100C
Epson – Expression 636 Artist 2

Such is the ever-changing, ever-improving nature of the computer peripherals market, including scanners, that it is difficult to supply a list of up-to-date equipment. Many computer and peripheral ranges have a lifespan measured in months or even weeks before they are replaced by newer, better, cheaper models.

However, we have done just that. The list given below is a selection of scanners available on the British market as this book went to press. It is neither exhaustive nor comprehensive but intends only to give an idea of what is available and approximately what it will cost. Remember that price is often a good indicator of build-quality and the quality of the software included with the scanner.

■ Umax – Astra 1220S

Although the Umax Astra 1220s is a SCSI-based scanner, it isn't as fast as it should be. This is due to its scanning mechanism. It takes so long to wind up and wind down that most parallel port scanners can beat it at nearly all tasks. However, it does have better than average image quality and is very versatile. Its price is possibly one of its redeeming factors because it functions like a scanner that should cost a lot more.

Resolution: 600 × 1200dpi

Colour Depth: 36-bit single pass (68,000 million colours)

Connection: SCSI-2

Bundled Software: PhotoDeluxe and PageManager

Price: £146

■ Hewlett Packard – ScanJet 6200C

The ScanJet 6200C can generate quality scans with minimal work. It seems to be aimed at business users who demand high quality scans and a certain degree of control over the images produced by the scanner. It's easy to use, very powerful and can be used as a one-touch copier with the help of HP's free ScanJet utility. The ease of use is due to its automation intelligence, which helps the user produce scans by trying to detect different aspects of the image that need to be scanned. The ScanJet does this while still maintaining a high level of control for the advanced user.

Resolution 600 × 1200

Colour Depth: 36-bit (68,000 million colours)

Connection: USB and SCSI

Bundled Software: OmniPage LE OCR, PhotoDeluxe II, PrecisionScan Lite, CreataCard

Price: £278

■ Canon – CanoScan FB 620

The CanoScan is a flatbed, colour and monochrome scanner that is designed for Windows 98, so it is uncertain whether it runs smoothly under Windows 95 or not. It is however a superb scanner that has four modes of operation: colour, greyscale, black and white, and text enhanced. It has a compact and stylish design, which is perfect for the home or small office and is very easy to install. It also has the advantage of having the Canon LIDE technology, which helps it produce crisp, sharp images. However, the only problem is that there are no accessories and it doesn't come with the bonus functions that are included in most scanners. For example, you can't connect another USB peripheral (like a printer) to the same port as the scanner. If you are running low on ports, then this could prove to be a problem.

Resolution: 600 × 600 dpi.

Colour Depth: single pass 36-bit internal

Connection: USB

Bundled Software: iPhoto Express, OmniPage LE

Price: £112

■ Umax – PowerLook III

The PowerLook is an expensive scanner. The price is justified, however, because it is one of the best scanners on the market. It's equipped with 12-bit A/D converters combined with Umax's Bit Enhancement Technology which adds another two bits. This combined with a colour depth of 42 bits (4.2 billion colours) makes this scanner a very powerful one indeed. The binuscan IPM (Image Processing Machine) corrects the colour of the scanned images with great efficiency. This enables the scanner to produce brilliant images first time. Another feature of this scanner is its batch scanning, you can highlight different areas of the original image, each with its own individual settings (such as colour options, size, resolution), and the scanner will scan them all automatically. However, it does suffer from a few problems: it needs a lot of temporary hard disk space (usually hundreds of megabytes) and although it can scan negatives, it doesn't do them very well. However, it is a good scanner (despite the price) and does come with a hot swap warranty where you get immediate replacement of the product if it malfunctions within the first year.

Resolution: 1200 × 2400 dpi

Colour Depth: 36-bit (69,000 million colours), 42-bit preprocessing (4.2 billion colours)

Connection: SCSI and ISA interface card

Bundled Software: Photoshop LE, BinuScan, PhotoPerfect Advanced, Xerox Textbridge, MagicScan

Price: £999

■ Agfa – SnapScan

SnapScan is a single-pass 24-bit colour flatbed scanner, which isn't bad, but compared to most scanners that are now 36-bit (and even 42-bit), it falls a little bit short. It has a removable lid that lets you scan books without trying to squeeze them under the cover. The SCSI cable is rather short (2 feet) and could cause problems if your PC is stored under or behind a desk. Unlike some of the manufacturers in this chapter, though, Agfa offers some optional accessories to the SnapScan. These include an automatic document feeder and a transparency adaptor. The former lets you store up to 60 sheets in its input tray, while the latter lets you scan slides and overheads by placing a light source above the CCD.

Resolution: 300 × 300 dpi

Colour Depth: 24-bit (16.7 million colours)

Connection: SCSI-2

Bundled Software: OmniPage LE OCR, PhotoImpact SE, SoftCopy, Copy it, FotoSnap, FotoLook

Price: £116

■ Hewlett Packard – ScanJet 4100C

Although the ScanJet 4100C has less than impressive colour output quality, its greyscale scans are reasonably good. Its colours are slightly dull, but the images are quite crisp and clean. Like the Astra 1220S, the 4100C has a scanning mechanism that slows it down despite its support for fast USB data transfer. However it does come with a good software bundle and a very competitive price. It also does a good job of automatically adjusting resolution settings, which can also be done manually, which makes it good for the novice and the more experienced user.

Resolution: 300 × 600 dpi

Colour Depth: 30-bit (1,073 million colours)

Connection: SCSI-2

Bundled Software: OmniPage LE OCR, PhotoDeluxe II, PrecisionScan Lite, CreataCard

Price: £92

■ Epson – Expression 636 Artist 2

This scanner is probably best suited to professionals. It has many functions including automatic or manual scanning. Setting it up is a very easy task and usually presents no problems. It has brilliant colour matching techniques such as closed loop calibration. Its biggest problem is that it is very difficult to use. However, once you have mastered its drivers, it becomes a very powerful tool for clean crisp images. It's tools for image editing and manipulation are very good and with them, you can achieve some impressive results. This is due to its best feature: the SilverFast interface.

Resolution: 600 × 600 dpi

Colour Depth: 36-bit (69,000 million colours)

Connection: SCSI

Price: approximately £400

Index